ENDORSEMENTS

Rockelle Lerner, author of *Daily Affirmations for Children of Alcoholics, Affirmations for the Inner Child, Living in the Comfort Zone* and *Connect with you Inner Spiritual Center*

> Patricia Hasting's book is a remarkable and inspiring journey that takes the reader into the joy and the mystery of synchronicity. I would recommend this book for anyone exploring their spirituality and their limitless potential for Divine guidance.

Lisa Tener, author of *The Ultimate Guide to Transforming Anger*

> This book made a profound impact on my life. In a way, Pat's inspiring stories have become my own. The evening after I read the first few chapters, I found myself telling some of the stories to my husband, son and mother-in-law—just gushing to share the power of the answers God had given Pat—and the beautiful ways that God has answered her prayers. Anyone searching for proof that God loves us— and that God truly is in the details—will find inspiration, laughter, love and hope in this beautiful book.

Donna Mac, Vital Women Radio

> Pat so beautifully lets us walk with her, feeling God's presence every step of the way. This book is a great reminder that if we simplify our busy lives, we too can turn His messages into great actions.

Joanne Di Bello, Director of Marketing URI

> I have always believed that Pat is the most faithful person I know. Her spirituality is such that she lives under the veil of unconditional trust. Her book is a testimony of that faith and trust. With the turn of each page, the miracles in her life unfold.

Simply a Woman
~ of Faith ~

How to Live in Spiritual Power
and Transform Your Life

Simply a Woman
of Faith

How to Live in Spiritual Power
and Transform Your Life

PAT HASTINGS

MILL CITY PRESS

For more information contact :
Mill City Press, Inc.
212 3rd Avenue North
Suite 570
Minneapolis, MN 55401
or info@millcitypress.net

www.millcitypress.net

ISBN - 1-934248-38-x

ISBN - 978-1-934248-38-6

LCCN: 2007932684

This book is dedicated to my
mother, Honey, and to the divine
Mother, Mary, who both reside in
the heavens and in my heart.

Contents

Acknowledgments

I am grateful to the Divine Presence which inspired and guided this book

To all the special people in my life who share my good times and brighten my days, I say thank you. You have been there to cheer me on when I didn't believe in myself and wanted to quit. Whether you are still an active part of my life or have gone on to continue your individual journey, you hold a special place in my heart.

My loving children: Brian, Tim, Mary and Jimmy. My daughter-in-law Suzie and grandchildren Zack and Josh

My friends: Carole Gaulin, Joanne Di bello, Gail Mills, Sandra Slonim, Kathy Orme, Laurie Boggs, Donna Mac for their loving support and encouragement

Paula Bernsfeld for praying for me and buying the book before it was published

My spiritual group: Ann Haviland, Karen Lucarelli, Michele Shea, Julie Palazini for believing in me and cheering me on

Lisa Tener for coaching and editing my book

Dayna Mondella for introducing me to Rebirthing and the breathwork community

Saisha Harris for creating the beautiful Angel cover for my book

My friends in Toastmasters –showing me how to be a better speaker and find my voice

Lloyd Slonim for creating my web page

Kathy Burroughs for patiently answering my computer questions

Ron Lussier for his photography

Ann Murphy and Sandy Derecktor for proofreading my manuscript

Pat Sears, dearest friend

~ *Introduction* ~

Simply a Woman of Faith is an inspirational, empowering memoir of my journey with God. The stories are a combination of "how-to" and "how-I" was provided for and divinely led. A journal question is provided at the end of each chapter. You will have the opportunity to go within and discover how God has worked in your life. You need not read the chapters in order; they are self contained and can be used in prayer or read at your leisure. Each chapter depicts an area of my life where God has led me, nurtured me, and provided everything I needed, often in miraculous ways.

You don't have to go through any challenge alone; the spirit of God within is your strength, your life, your courage and your serenity. What you cannot do for yourself, God will do. God will "show up" in his perfect time and perfect way.

In this book, you will learn:

✟ How to connect with the Divine and find the sacred place within your soul where there is perfect peace.

✟ How to transform your fears and live in Divine-spiritual power.

✟ How God communicates with you in a language that is understood by your soul, learning to hear God's small still voice within.

✟ How to strengthen your faith in God and receive His abundance and blessings.

✟ How to let go of problems and place them in Gods loving hands, trusting the unfolding of a Divine Plan.

✟ How to become a free, healthy, joyful, inspired expression of God.

✟ How to receive Divine Love and radiate God's love to the world.

✝ How to develop an intimate relationship with God through daily prayer and meditation.

✝ How to practice loving patience and wait for God's perfect plan to unfold.

✝ How to recognize and be open to GODincidences in your life.

✝ How to connect with your passion and create your dream.

I am honored and blessed to share my spiritual journey with you. My deepest desire is to share God's love and faithfulness with you. God has worked miracles in the details of my everyday life. As a result, I am a woman with deep faith. Through prayer and meditation, God persistently and lovingly guided me every step of the way and gave me everything I needed when I needed it. When I took a detour and allowed fear to rob me and almost destroy God's gift within me, God always led me back to His loving presence. What I needed always "showed up" in God's perfect timing and in His perfect way.

Writing the book has taught me to trust the process and God's perfect timing. It's taught me to be patient and wait, knowing that all is in Divine timing. I'm grateful and my heart overflows that God has chosen me to be His instrument of love and healing.

Doors have opened that I never dreamed would open. Writing *Simply a Woman of Faith* has changed me from the inside out. I am a new woman transformed and healed by Divine love.

I've faced myself, my fears and learned to trust and believe in myself and God's promise. I used to look to others for answers. Now I go within for my own wisdom, intuition and answers. I trust the peace of God within as His gift of guidance.

When I started writing *Simply a Woman of Faith* seven years ago, I heard the small still voice of God say:

DO YOUR PART AND LEAVE THE OUTCOME TO ME. THIS IS MY PLAN AND I WILL ACCOMPLISH IT.

I've done my part and now I let go of the outcome. *Simply a Woman of Faith* is in God's hands.

In sharing my personal stories and opening my heart, I hope to show you:

✝ How God guides us

✛ How He communicates with us

✛ How He provides and

✛ How to follow God's will in your life

God "shows up" in the smallest details of our lives when we ask for what we want and need. The first chapter provides examples of my yard sale forays and answered prayers. God "shows up" in profound miraculous ways which I will share in later chapters.

I

God is My
Bargain Hunter

How God Provides at Yard Sales

My favorite thing to do on a Saturday morning is to go what I term "yard sailing." I love the thrill of a bargain and haggling for the best price. I always pray and ask God to provide for what I need. When my prayers are answered, I feel loved and cared for.

Please God, don't let me buy anything that I don't need. And, don't forget I need a vacuum cleaner today.

On Friday night, I circle all the yard sales in the newspaper that are close by. The neighborhood yard sales are the most fun. Cars line the roads and people go from house to house looking for chairs for their dining room table, a microwave, clothes for the new baby or just browsing for a fun buy. I'm dressed and out the door by seven thirty in the morning because I don't want to miss that eight slice toaster that toasts bagels or the bike rack for my car. I often spot the yard sale sign blocks before I even reach it. I can't stand a sign so small I can't read it. Even worse is following a sign for miles, only to find out that the yard sale was last week and they forgot to take the sign down.

Fortunately, my last minute turns to follow a yard sale that was posted too close to the turn have never caused an accident. I do get a few beeps and a dirty look or two. To anyone I've scared, I do apologize.

My friends call me the "yard sale queen." Whenever they need something, they ask me to look for it. They tell me what they want and how much they want to spend.

"Pat, would you look for a three quart pressure cooker when you go to the yard sale today?" my friend Joanne asked one day. "I have a two quart pressure cooker, but my in-laws are visiting and I want to make a big stew tomorrow that requires a three quart cooker. I don't want to spend more than three dollars, max."

"I'll keep my eyes peeled." I replied.

God, you are going to have to help me with this one. I didn't even know they made three quart pressure cookers.

I found the pressure cooker the same day Joanne asked. I can usually tell if it's a good yard sale –worth the stop – from the road. As I slowed to look, I thought this particular yard sale looked like a junker - clothes and toys strewn everywhere. I started to pull away when a metal object caught my eye.

Is that a pressure cooker on the table? It sure looks like one. I parked my car and walked over to examine it. Not just any old pressure cooker. This one held three quarts. I didn't want to look too interested as the woman walked over to me to tell me the price.

"How much are you asking for this?" I asked.

"Six dollars."

"Will you take three for it?"

"Do you know how expensive these are in the store?" she answered.

"Yes, but will you take three for it? It's for a friend and that's all she wants to spend."

"Okay," she halfheartedly replied.

I paid and quickly grabbed my find before she could change her mind.

Thank you God, Joanne will be thrilled when I bring this to her later in the day.

"You always dress well. Where do you shop?" my friend Linda asked. I smiled and bragged "yard sales and consignment stores." I love to find something that fits flawlessly in one yard sale and then find something that matches perfectly at the next yard sale. It's better than shopping in department stores and it's a hell of a lot cheaper. My coworkers know I shop at yard sales and always ask on Monday mornings, "Pat, did you get that at a yard sale?" They try to guess how much I paid. "Did you pay fifty cents?"

I just smile and nod my head.

I started going to yard sales many years ago out of necessity. My husband was out of work for a year. There wasn't enough money for the basics for the two of us and our four small children. I found my children's clothes at my weekly yard sales. The clothes almost looked brand new after I brought them home and washed them. While they were young, the children never knew the clothes came from yard sales and I could get away with it. When they got older, I had to sneak the stuff into the house so they wouldn't know where they came from.

My faith was strengthened whenever God answered a prayer request and I found just what I was looking for.

God's most stupendous yard sale miracle

God, Joe needs shoes for his job interview. You know we can't afford $150 for a new pair of black wing tip shoes. I know this is not the usual request and it may take awhile to find since he's a size 12D. I trust you God.

God must look down and smile at some of my unique prayer requests. A size 12D man's shoe was a tall order, even for God. This didn't happen overnight, but I didn't give up. I kept praying, asking and going to yard sales. One of these days, I'll find them, I thought to myself.

I did a double take when I walked into the yard sale and spotted boxes of shoes stacked neatly on the table. I raced over to the table, my heart pounding loudly. I carefully opened all the boxes hoping to find size 12 D black wing tip shoes. It didn't look like they had any large sizes and I was about to give up. With that, a man walked over to me and asked if I needed help.

"You don't have what I'm looking for," I responded.

"What do you need?"

I kind of chuckled and said, "I need size 12D man's shoes – preferably, black wing tips."

"Wait a minute, I think I have some larger sizes over here. Follow me." I held my breath anticipating what we might find. He opened all the boxes searching for a 12D.

"Yes, here we go. Is this what you are looking for?" He held up a shiny pair of black wing tip, 12D.

"I could hardly get the words out of my mouth. "Are you sure they're a size 12D?"

"Yes, lady. The size is right here. Look, size 12D." He pointed to the size marking on the inner leather.

"How much?"

He thought about it for a moment and then said, "Twenty five dollars will do."

"It's a deal, I'll take them."

God's love and care never cease to amaze me and I wanted to shout it from the housetops. I couldn't hold back and blurted out, "I'm so happy I came here today. My husband is out of work and has a job interview next week. He didn't have any dress shoes and he couldn't afford to buy new ones. I've been praying to find new shoes at a yard sale. I knew God would answer my prayers."

He looked at me kindly and said, "I sold my shoe store a year ago. These shoes were leftovers. They weren't doing me any good in the basement and I just wanted to get rid of them. Glad you found what you were looking for."

I paid for the shoes and thanked him. I couldn't wait to get home and have my husband try them on.

I ran into the house and shouted to my husband, "guess what? I found new shoes for you at a yard sale—and they're wing tips."

He looked a bit apprehensive at first, but smiled and sat down to try them on.

I held my breath as I watched him slip his foot into the shoe. Just like Cinderella, the shoe fit like a glove. God is faithful. He wants to provide for His children. We need to only ask and believe.

The five hats prayer request

God, I need five hats and I need them today. Where am I going to find hats now? I don't want to spend a lot of money on them. The retreat is next weekend so this can't wait.

Over several months, I had amassed fifteen old fashioned women's hats for the fifteen women who signed up for my retreat. We dress up for a talent show on Saturday night. At the last minute, five more women signed up and I didn't have enough hats to go around.

That day, I took my time browsing at all the yard sales and eventually forgot all about looking for hats. I stopped dead in my tracks when I spotted the colorful hats from a distance.

I quickly walked over to check out the hats on the table, hoping they would be what I wanted. The hats were perfect for the retreat —hats from the forties—several with veils and other sporting big colored flowers. My favorite was the Jackie Kennedy style black velvet pill box. I picked out the prettiest hats. The best part was the price—two bucks each. *Thank you God for answering this prayer.*

God is interested in the smallest details of our lives. He wants us to ask so He can provide.

I don't always know I need something until I see it. As I walked around the yard sale, my eyes were drawn to the brand new jewelry box sitting on the table. *This is perfect to keep my jewelry neat on my dresser, rather than the mess I have scattered about.* It stood about eighteen inches high and had five drawers. I would have a place for everything – my earrings, necklaces and bracelets.

"How much is the jewelry box?" I asked the women who approached me.

"It's fifteen dollars."

"Will you take five?"

"No, I want fifteen. It's brand new."

"Thanks, but I don't want to spend that much at a yard sale."

I'll go back at the end of the day and see if it's still there. If it doesn't sell, she'll be happy to take five dollars.

Now that I could picture in my head how neat my dresser would look, I really obsessed about the jewelry box. I couldn't wait to go back at the end of the day and see if it was still there. As I drove down the long block, I squinted to see if was still there.

Yeah, it's still there. This is my day. I'm sure she'll take five dol-

lars now. *I hope she doesn't remember me from this morning.* I didn't waste any time and walked right up to the lady.

"Will you take five dollars for the jewelry box?" She wasn't budging.

"No, I'll take fifteen, it's brand new and still in the box. I'll keep it for myself if I can't get fifteen."

With a look of defeat on my face, I said, "Thank you" and walked away. It's the principle at yard sales. You're not supposed to spend a lot of money for other people's junk. But, clearly, this wasn't junk. Maybe I was just being cheap. I guess she really didn't want to sell it after all.

When I returned home and looked at my messy dresser, I felt disappointed that the lady wouldn't sell the jewelry box for five dollars.

God, maybe next Saturday I'll find a nice one - a jewelry box with drawers so I can be organized.

I noticed the yard sale sign on the pole as I returned home from church the next day. *I'll ride by quickly and see if they have a jewelry box,* I thought to myself. I didn't even get out of my car because all I saw was antiques. I started to drive away; then stopped my car and backed up. There in the middle of the table among all the antiques was an eight drawer mahogany jewelry box. Not only did it have more drawers, but it matched the mahogany wood on my dresser. I got out of my car feeling hopeful. The price was right—four bucks. I couldn't wait to get home and clean out my old jewelry box.

A walking cast prayer request

My daughter Mary called me and said, "Mom, I broke my foot last night."

"What happened? Are you okay?" I asked anxiously.

"I fell down the cellar stairs, but I'm okay."

"Did you get an x- ray?"

"No, I'll be all right mom. Don't worry. "Can you get me a walking cast at the hospital?"

"They don't have them there." I replied. "I'll go to the hospital supply store tomorrow after I go yard sailing and buy you one."

"Thanks mom. See you tomorrow."

I sure wish she'd get an x-ray, but she's thirty years old and is going to do it her way, I reminded myself.

The walking cast was the furthest thing from my mind as I strolled around this particular yard sale. I bought a few things for the house and paid the lady when out of the corner of my eye, I spotted it.

God, am I seeing right? That looks like a walking cast sitting there in the middle of the driveway.

"Excuse me, but is that a walking cast over there?"

"Yes, I bought it for my husband a few years ago and he never used it."

"Oh, how much are you asking for it?"

"One dollar."

"Sold."

I walked out of the yard sale with a smile on my face and a skip in my step. I drove straight to Mary's house. I couldn't wait to tell her the good news. I hurried into her house and found her sitting with her leg propped up on the living room couch.

"Mary, guess what? I found a walking cast at a yard sale, try it on and see if it fits."

"It fits perfectly." It didn't take her long before she was up and wobbling around.

An air conditioner prayer request

My air conditioner broke on one of the hottest days of the summer. I didn't want to buy a new one and spend the money if I didn't have to. *Maybe Carole has one lying around her basement she isn't using,* I thought to myself. *I'll ask her when I get to her house.*

God, I need an air conditioner and I would like to get it free. I prayed while driving to Carole's. I just finished the prayer when I spotted the air conditioner sitting on the side of the street. It looked like it was put out for trash day.

God, is this you? Should I ring the doorbell and ask if I can have it if it works? Why not, I thought to myself. I slowly walked up the driveway and knocked on the door.

"Hi, I noticed you have an air conditioner on the side of the street. Does it work?"

"Yes, it does. I bought a new one and didn't need this one anymore," she replied.

"Do you mind if I take it? Mine just broke today."

"Sure, you can have it; it's heavy though. Let me call my husband and he can put it in your car."

"Thank you very much," I answered.

Not only does God provide, but He sends angels to help along the way.

A baby carrier prayer request

I had two specific prayer requests that I wanted to find at the yard sales this one particular day. My daughter asked for a baby carrier for the back of her bike for her birthday. Her new puppy wanted to go for rides with her. As I browsed around the yard sale, I noticed a partially opened box. I couldn't tell what it was because it was so well wrapped in bubble wrap.

"Excuse me, what is this wrapped in the box?"

"A bike carrier. We only used it a few times and it's in great shape."

"How much?" I asked.

"Thirty five dollars. We paid one hundred and fifty dollars for it a few years ago."

I smiled and said, "I'll take it."

The puppy loved riding on the back of the bike all around town.

Another request:

An air mattress prayer request

My second request was for a queen size air mattress for my son who was coming to my house for the weekend. I hadn't found it at the first yard sale. At the next one, I looked around and didn't see anything that looked like an air mattress either. A tall, slim woman came up to me and asked, "Is there something in particular that you're looking for?"

"Yes, I'm looking for a queen size air mattress, but I didn't see one here."

"Oh, you missed it. We have one right over here."

My son slept comfortably that weekend.

The beauty of my "yard sailing" lies not just in the price, but the knowledge that God does care about the details. His answers to my yard sale prayers constantly reminds me that I'm taken care of, that God is in my life and that He wants me to have all I need and desire. The fun I have finding these bargains reminds me that God has fun when I have fun. I think God enjoys placing bargains in my path as much as I enjoy finding them.

I Am a Woman Giving Birth to Myself

JOURNAL PAGE

Do I ask God for what I want and need? If not, why not?

_____

_____

_____

_____

_____

_____

_____

_____

_____

_____

_____

_____

_____

_____

_____

_____

_____

_____

_____

_____

II

Help Me
≈ *to Believe* ≈

How God Guides Through Open & Closed Doors

My life changed thirty years ago when I walked into that little bookstore. On that day, my browsing led me to a small book called *How God Guides Us* (Manna Christian Outreach, Basham, 1975.) Tucked away on the back of the wooden bookshelf, I almost missed the tiny book with one hundred pages.

Only a buck, I thought silently - I couldn't resist the bargain. When I returned home that day, I read it from cover to cover in two hours.

When I don't know if something is God's will or my will, I pray, "God open or close the door." It hurts when the door is slammed in my face and I'm left wandering in the hallway until the next door opens. God must get a chuckle when I'm banging and pleading with Him to do something. Here's where the trust and faith come in.

"Closed doors are a valid part of guidance. When God closes a door, it's because there is another plan, a better plan. If He closes one door, He'll open another – according to His timing, not mine. I keep moving in faith, even in the face of closed doors." —(Basham, 1975)

I may be guided to do one thing and then when I get there, God has something else in mind. He doesn't tell me His full plan ahead of time, which is probably good. That's His way. Mine is to love, trust and follow.

Guidance comes when I move in faith, not when I sit in doubt. I step out in faith, trusting that if I make a mistake, God will correct it and get me back on the right path for my life. I've made plenty of mistakes along the way, but I have always been protected and led back to where I need to be. It's not easy to hear God in the midst of our busy lives. Sometimes, it doesn't make sense and I question if I am really hearing God or not. When I'm faithful in listening to the seemingly small things, I will be led in more important ways. For example, the next incident my listening didn't seem important, but it turned out to be the right thing to do.

Walking into the building from the parking lot where I work, I heard the small still voice of God say:

GO IN ANOTHER DOOR.

But God, I'm already late, why do I have to go in another door? What difference does it make what door I go in? I silently argued. Will I miss something important if I don't listen? I wondered.

I reluctantly turned around and headed for the other door.

God, is this my imagination? What is it I'm supposed to learn or do?

As I hurried back to my office, I heard over the loud speaker that the meeting I needed to attend was starting in five minutes.

Oh, that's right, the meeting. Thank you God for reminding me.

I forgot all about the meeting and would have missed it if I'd gone in the other door and missed the announcement. Once in the door, I ran into my co-worker Donna with whom I'd been playing phone tag for several days. We talked face to face about the patient who recently overdosed on heroin and was in the intensive care unit. This wouldn't have happened if I walked through the other door.

God is not only interested in guiding us in the big things in our lives, but the small ones as well. Do you listen, even when it doesn't make sense?

God acts as my real estate agent

God, what should I do? I don't want to make a mistake. Please help me. What is your will for me? I have to make up my mind, whether to sell or re-mortgage my house.

I could no longer afford the high monthly mortgage payment because of my impending divorce. I didn't want to sell my house and would do anything to stay there. My mind was like a blender, and I couldn't find the off button. One minute, I was moving and the next I was staying. If I re-mortgaged, I could get a lower interest rate and could then afford the monthly payments.

God, please guide me to make the right decision, I quietly prayed. When I finally made the decision to re-mortgage, the peace came. My soon to be ex-husband agreed to sign the necessary papers. On the morning of the closing, he called and said, "Sorry, but I changed my mind and cannot sign the papers." I couldn't speak at first, as the fear rose up in my throat.

This can't be happening. I must not be hearing him right.

"You have to sign them," I shouted over the phone hysterically. "I won't be able to keep the house if I don't re-mortgage now."

I couldn't talk him out of it, no matter what I said. His mind was made up. I called the bank to ask if I could sign the papers without my husband's signature. "No." He had to sign the papers because his name was on the house. The closing was cancelled.

God, I don't understand, I trusted you were guiding me. Did I hear you wrong? Why did you allow me to go through all of this only to close the door at the last minute?

I don't like it when my faith is tested.

Can I trust you God? I want to believe you closed the door for a reason and there is something better for me, but I'm having a hard time trusting now.

A week later, to my surprise, I received a letter from the mortgage company informing me that the interest rate had gone down (on its own) because it was an adjustable mortgage. The payment was the same as if I had re-mortgaged. I even saved a few thousand dollars in the process. God closed the door (through my ex's husband's last minute postponement) to save me money. When I walk in faith, God always provides in His way and His time.

Several years later, I made the decision to sell my house and rent a condo. The idea of renting a condo appealed to me because I didn't like all the work that came along with owning my own home. I thought it would take months to sell the house because houses weren't moving at all. It clearly wasn't a seller's market.

I can take my time and leisurely look for something that is afford-able and close to work, I thought to myself.

My house sold in three days! Not only did I have one offer, but two. When it rains, it pours and I was flying high until reality set in. I didn't have a place to live, and I had to be out in eight weeks.

God, what am I going to do now? Where am I going to live? I don't know where to even start.

I looked in the newspaper the next day. To my surprise, there were several condos in the area for rent. Off I went with newspaper in hand, determined to find a condo that day. As I drove along a street lined with big old oak trees, I got excited about the first house before even seeing it. I could ride my bike to work if I wanted to. A woman with grey hair pulled back in a bun answered the door.

"Hi, I'm Millie Olsen, you must be Pat Hastings, come right in."

"Thanks," I answered and entered into the foyer.

She gave me a tour of the house and I instantly fell in love with the very large rooms and hardwood floors. The patio in the back with the flower garden and blooming red roses sealed it for me. I put a deposit down that day. I knew in my heart that God had led me there.

I went home, started packing boxes and throwing things away. My four children grew up in this house so there were many senti-mental things that I didn't want to part with.

How did I ever accumulate all of this stuff, I wondered. *What do I keep and what do I throw away? I can't throw away my kid's birthday cards to me, or the gifts they gave me over the years, can I?* Things were going along fine until…

Four weeks prior to the settlement, I received a phone call from my real estate agent.

"Pat, are you sitting down, I have some bad news for you."

"Oh"

God, I really don't want to hear any bad news.

I held my breath and clenched my fist tightly as I waited for him to tell me the bad news.

"The woman backed out of the deal due to some technicality in the agreement."

"I can't believe that. Can she do that legally?"

"Yes, Pat, I'm afraid she has the right to do it. I'm sorry, but the deal is off."

"What am I going to do now? I've already paid a deposit plus first month's rent on the condo."

"We can put the house back on the market immediately and hope for the best."

It felt like I couldn't breathe and I wanted to throw up, as I sat there and sobbed.

That's easy for him to say. He's not in my shoes. I'll never be able to sell it in four weeks and be in the condo on time. My house is in total shambles with boxes piled high in all the rooms. No one will buy it like this. God, where are you and what are you doing? I want to trust you God because you have never let me down, but this doesn't look good. Help me to believe.

I calmed down by taking a deep breath, and remembering God's timing is perfect. I prayed and asked for help.

God, you're in control. I trust you. I don't know what the future will bring, but I do know that I will be okay, no matter what. As I sat there and meditated, I heard God's voice say:

PAT, CALL THE FIRST COUPLE WHO MADE A BID ON THE HOUSE.

They were from out of state and also wanted to settle in eight weeks.

Maybe they haven't found a house yet.

I could feel the excitement bubbling up inside of me. My hands trembled as I dialed the phone to call my real estate agent.

"John, I have a great idea and wished I'd thought of it sooner."

"What's that, Pat?"

"Will you call the couple who made a bid on the house and see if they are still interested in buying my house?"

God, I don't ask you much, but I'm asking you to please let them say " yes."

I didn't hear for several days and it seemed like an eternity. I didn't sleep much because my mind wouldn't shut off.

What am I going to do if they say"no?"

Finally, the call came—I waited with bated breath for the verdict.

"Pat, I have good news for you. The couple wants to buy your house and can move in within four weeks."

"That's great news. What happened?"

"They hadn't found a house yet and were planning on moving in with his parents until they could find a house they liked. And, by the way, they're thrilled."

We settled exactly four weeks to the day, and I happily moved into the condo right on time. Another "GODincidence." My faith is strengthened each time I trust God and His perfect timing. The more impossible things look, the more God is glorified.

I Am a Woman Giving Birth to Myself

JOURNAL PAGE

Is there a time in my life when God opened or closed a door? How did it feel? If God closed a door, how did it feel at first? Did you feel differently later on, when you saw how things turned out?

_____

_____

_____

_____

_____

_____

_____

_____

_____

_____

_____

_____

_____

_____

_____

_____

_____

_____

III

God Speaks

How God Speaks in Our Lives

Is there someone here who needs Your love, God?

Newport is a stone's throw away from my home in Providence, Rhode Island and a great place to get away and just be. My spirit is renewed and I feel energized whenever I take a trip to the ocean. I sit mesmerized by the power of the ocean, as I watch the waves rush in and out, crashing over the rocks.

As I drove across the Newport bridge for my weekend R&R, I prayed to be led and open to God's spirit. Thoughts of my graduation day lingered in my mind. What a thrill it was to walk across the stage and receive my bachelor's degree at the age of 44. I felt grateful for God's love and presence in my life, and I wanted to share it with someone, especially someone who needed to hear they were loved.

God please lead me. I want to do Your will.

I settled into my room and took a late morning nap before heading out to lunch to my favorite restaurant overlooking Narragansett Bay. I loved watching the boats and yachts come in and out as I sipped my lobster bisque.

After lunch, I plopped my beach chair at the edge of the ocean along First Beach, watching the world go by. When I got bored, I took a long walk along the beach. The hot sun felt nourishing and the ocean breeze kept me just cool enough. All weekend long, I listened in my heart to hear God's voice. But I heard nothing.

I'm disappointed God. I wanted to meet someone and share your love with them, but it's almost time to go home. Maybe I missed something.

I drove out to the ocean one more time before leaving, still quietly hoping God would lead me to someone.

As I drove my car along the ocean road, I clearly and loudly heard,

PULL OVER HERE.

I quickly turned off the road and parked in the parking lot. I eagerly walked to the ocean, sensing God was at work. There were many people and children sitting on the rocks, playing ball and enjoying the sunshine and warm summer breeze.

Okay God, now what? Is there someone here who needs to know Your love?

YES! I heard quietly in my spirit. As I scanned the area, I noticed a woman sitting by herself on the rocks. She looked immersed in her own thoughts. Deep in my heart, I knew she was the one God wanted me to talk to.

What do I say? What will she think of me? Am I nuts? Maybe this is all in my head and I should just go back to my car. I couldn't; I felt compelled, propelled to follow through.

I know I asked You to lead me God. Why am I afraid and doubting You now?

My heart pounded. I nervously walked over, stuck out my hand and introduced myself. I didn't waste any time, because I knew if I did, I may have chickened out.

"Hi. I'm Pat Hastings."

Looking at me kind of strangely she said, "I'm Susan."

"Susan, God wants you to know that He loves you very much."

Her jaw dropped. I could see that my words had taken her off guard. Yet, nothing came out of her mouth. I'm sure she wondered, "Who is this woman and where did she come from?"

The color drained from her face, and she stared at me in shock and disbelief. Tears rolled slowly down her cheeks. Then, the flood gates opened up as she sobbed uncontrollably and her body shook. I wasn't expecting this kind of raw emotion and didn't know what to do to comfort her.

God, I need help. What do I do now?

I gently put my hand on her shoulder and silently prayed. I realized I didn't have to do anything, but just be there with her. It seemed like an eternity before she got herself together and calmed down. As she looked into my eyes, the words came tumbling out, as if we knew each other for years.

"I want to die. I wanted to kill myself at the very moment you arrived."

I gasped, trying to keep my cool.

"Why? What happened?" I nervously asked her.

"My husband cheated on me and left me for another woman. We were married for twenty five years and I thought we had a good marriage. I don't know how I can go on without him. I was so distraught that I missed a few weeks of work. My boss called me into his office yesterday and fired me. I'm better off dead."

My heart went out to her as I reached out for her hand.

"I'm sorry for your pain, Susan. God sent me here today to tell you He loves you. God wants to help you. He knows your pain and what you're going through."

Her body relaxed and her face lightened as she intently listened to my words.

"I thought God abandoned me too – that I was being punished for something. I desperately need to know God loves me and I'm not alone. How can I thank you Pat for coming into my life today?"

We sat and talked for a long time about God's love and how He helped her in the past. She wanted to trust and believe He would do it again. God touched her heart and soul that day and slowly hope and confidence returned. Convinced God loved her, she found the courage to go on and face her problems. We thanked God together, both knowing our meeting was divinely appointed and a GODincidence. We kept in contact for a few years through telephone. Susan went back to school and became a kindergarten teacher, something she always wanted to do.

I can think of another occasion where God asked me to speak His words to someone. When planning my trip to Bangor, Maine, my hotel sent me an invitation in the mail to listen to a two hour-time share presentation. *It will be worth listening to the "spiel' to get the two free nights at another hotel in the future,* I told myself.

I had no intention of buying a time share and planned on being up front right away. If I told them the truth in the beginning, I wouldn't have to listen to the high-pressured sales pitch for too long. I sat patiently waiting for the salesperson to call my name, while thinking about the hot tub in the hotel.

"Hi, my name is Marsha Dione. Please follow me this way."

I liked her smile. She seemed pleasant and friendly. We sat down in a cramped cubicle in an office overlooking the mountains and she started her spiel. Before getting too far into her talk, I politely stopped her.

"Marsha, I want to be up front with you and not waste your time. I'm not going to buy a time share. I'm only here to claim the two free nights for listening to the talk. Besides, my dad owns a time share that I use every year so I don't need another one."

She looked stunned by my candor, but it didn't stop her. She wanted to make a sale.

"Thank you for your honesty. I appreciate it, but let me just tell you about…"

"Marsha, I would love to own a time share, but I can't afford one because I'm saving my money to buy a house."

"I understand. I just bought my own home and I know how long it takes to save the money." We chatted for awhile about houses and money. For whatever reason, she blurted out, "I worry constantly about money and not being able to pay the bills."

Somehow, the conversation turned to faith and trusting God to provide. I sensed in my spirit that she needed to talk. I listened.

"Marsha, I have an affirmation I say every day and it helps me a lot. Would you like to hear it?"

"Yes, I would."

"Everything I need is streaming toward me, I open my hands and receive."

"I can't believe you just said that. My father said almost the same words to me a few days ago. He's worried about me."

"Why?" I asked.

"He knows I'm struggling and having a difficult time with God."

That's interesting, I thought to myself and knew I had a captive audience. We needed to talk about God—and not about time shares.

"I'm having a hard time with God and a Higher Power," she confessed.

"Why?"

"I'm angry at God. I'm adopted and my real mother left me when I was only three months old. I have to find her and ask her why she abandoned me. And I won't give up until I find her."

"Are you angry at God because you can't find your mother?"

"Yes. My adoptive mother was a drunk and hated me. Because of that, I don't trust anyone, especially men. I attract men who are married and can't be there for me. I'm tired of it."

Why does she trust me, God? Is this a divine appointment?

Her face became beat red as she spoke. "I'm in a relationship with a married man who I work with. I know it's wrong and I feel guilty about it, but I'm afraid to leave and be alone. I hate myself for who I've become."

I wanted to help her. She needed God's healing touch if she was ever going to be free. We shared openly and she seemed to feel better as she unloaded her past and shook her burdens off her shoulders. Her somber mood seemed to change, and I saw a glimmer of hope in her eyes.

Sitting up straight in her chair, and with a proud look on her face, she announced,

"I'm a recovering drug addict and sober for one year. I work hard at my recovery and never want to go back to drugging again."

"Marsha, that's great. Good for you."

She stopped talking for a minute, as if pondering something important.

"Many of my co-workers are Christian. They invited me to go out with them. I always say, "No."

"Why?"

"They want to pray with me and I'm afraid. I avoid them like the plague."

I trusted it was a GODincidence and that God opened the door for me to share His love with her. My heart went out to her as I looked deeply into her eyes and saw her pain. The words spilled out of me as I looked lovingly into her soul.

"Marsha, God sent me here to tell you that He loves you and wants to heal you." Her face softened and her eyes watered as she tried to hold back the tears.

"How could God love me when I'm in a relationship with a married man? I don't think God could ever forgive me."

"Yes, Marsha, He will forgive you and wants to help you. God is a forgiving God and when you turn from your wrongdoing, you will be forgiven."

You could see in her eyes that she desperately wanted the pain to go away and to know she was loved and could be forgiven.

"When you are alone tonight in your room, get on your knees and ask God for help and forgiveness."

As she looked down at the floor, and back up at me, she sheepishly said, "I don't know how to do that."

We burst out laughing and I showed her how to do it. I dropped to my knees right there in the middle of the room and said a short prayer. I didn't care who saw me. She looked aghast, but amused. When we were saying goodbye and hugging each other, she said, "Pat, I connected with you immediately when you smiled and shook my hand. Thank you for what you did for me today. I feel much better and will do what you told me to do tonight."

When I saw her the next day, she looked different and more at peace with herself.   She ran up to me, gave me a big hug and said, "I got on my knees last night and asked for forgiveness. I poured out my heart to God and released deep pain I didn't even know was there. I felt a peace and serenity I haven't felt for a very long time, if ever. My heart is lighter today. And guess what? I'm going out with my Christian friends tonight."

My desire is to do God's will in my life. Sinda Jordan in her book *Inspired by Angels* states "Know that God's will is made known to you by entering the silence and allowing your heart to guide you. Listen to the loving voice within your heart and you will no longer fear the decisions in your life. Trust your heart to bring God's counsel into every decision you make." (Blue Dolphin Publishing, Jordan.1995)

I want to listen to my intuition and to the small voice of God within. I struggle sometimes because I'm not sure if it's God's voice

or my own. God is persistent and keeps sending me the same message until I get it.

I recall another time I almost didn't listen to God, but thankfully,
He got through to me.

CALL ROSE AND TELL HER EVERYTHING IS GOING TO BE ALL RIGHT.

*But God, I haven't talked to her in seven years. I can't call her out
of the clear blue sky and tell her everything is going to be alright. What
if everything was already alright? She's going to think I'm nuts.*

Rose and I had lost touch with one another after she moved to
Vermont several years earlier. I missed her, even though we didn't
see one another much when she lived close by. We didn't talk for
months, but when we did connect, it felt like we had never left each
other. We shared our spiritual journey and what really mattered
in our lives. Still, it had been seven long years. How could I just
call her out of the blue and pretend to know she was going through
something? Again, the small still voice of God whispered in my ear.

CALL ROSE

Okay God, I get the message, I'll call. I slowly dialed her telephone number, secretly hoping she wouldn't answer, as if you can
keep a secret from God.

"Hi Rose, this is Pat."

"Oh my God, I can't believe it's you, Pat. How are you?"

"I'm fine." I blurted out God's message as quickly as I could.

"Rose, God wants you to know that everything is going to work
out all right in your life."

Dead silence. Then I heard her voice quiver, as she began to
speak.

"I'm going through a tough time, trying to discern God's will for
my life. I feel confused and anxious. I'm being asked to make a ma-
jor life change in my ministry and I'm scared to death that I won't
be able to do it."

She poured out her heart and in between sentences, she kept
repeating,

"I can't believe you called. I needed to hear this message."

When she was done she asked, "What's going on with you? How
are the kids? How's your job? Have you met anyone yet? I answered

all her questions and when we were both satisfied that we'd caught up, we said goodbye and hung up, promising to keep in touch.

Thank you God for allowing me to listen and reach out to my friend. She really needed me today.

Six months later, Rose came to my home for dinner. After we greeted each other warmly, I could tell she wanted to tell me what happened after our conversation.

"Pat, I can't wait to tell you what happened after we talked six months ago. When I hung up the phone after your call, I immediately felt peaceful. The fear and anxiety were gone. I knew deep down in my heart that everything was going to be fine. The peace of God sustained me through the discerning process. And like God promised, everything worked out perfectly."

CALL LINDA AND TELL HER I LOVE HER.

Linda kept popping into my mind as I lay awake in bed at three o'clock in the morning. She had attended one of my retreats and I hadn't seen her in months.

I'm not going to call her now God. Do you know it's three in the morning? I need my sleep and I bet she does too.

I prayed for her and went back to sleep. When I woke up the next morning, there it was again, the small still voice of God:

CALL LINDA AND TELL HER I LOVE HER.

The thought kept persisting. That's usually a sign for me to move ahead. I trusted that if it wasn't God, the door would be closed. Her answering machine picked up and I left a message for her to call me back. Several days went by and she still hadn't returned my phone call. I called and left another message.

God, do you want me to talk to her? I feel funny calling her again. This must be a closed door. Maybe it wasn't your voice after all. I guess I'm supposed to just pray for her.

I trusted the door was closed for a reason. Did God want to see if I'd listen and do what He was asking, despite my doubts? Several months later, Linda kept coming into my mind again. I prayed for her. I didn't plan on calling her again until I heard the small still voice of God say:

CALL HER AND SAY HELLO.

"Okay, God, I'll call her." I knew God would get His way, so I didn't argue.

"Hi Linda, how are you? I was thinking about you and just wanted to say hello."

"I'm feeling better than I have in a long time."

"Oh?"

"I'm praying on a daily basis." She then proceeded to tell me her story.

"A few months ago, I was at the lowest point in my life. Life had no meaning. I don't know what happened, but I suddenly started to feel God's love and presence. And I started to pray."

"Linda, I was praying for you at that time and asking God to bless you. I called you, but you didn't return my phone calls. I was going to tell you that God loved you."

Although I didn't get through to her on the phone, God heard the prayers. I believe God lifted her out of her despair and loved her into wholeness. I don't have to know how or why things happen as they do. I just need to listen to God, do my part and leave the rest to Him.

I Am a Woman Giving Birth to Myself

JOURNAL PAGE

When did someone's word or deed have an impact on my life?
When did I have an impact on someone else?

_____

_____

_____

_____

_____

_____

_____

_____

_____

_____

_____

_____

_____

_____

_____

_____

_____

_____

_____

_____

_____

IV

Buy It and
~ *I Will Provide* ~

How Does God Guide Us

"What a pretty blouse," my friend Amy said as she touched the silky sleeve of my pink blouse.

"Thanks. It's my God-blouse," I replied.

I love to tell the story of my God-blouse, a top I bought twenty years ago during a difficult time. My husband had been unemployed for a year, and we had four children under the age of ten. I swallowed my pride and applied for food stamps and welfare.

I will never forget the feeling of humiliation when I stood in line waiting at the welfare office.

God, I'm so embarrassed. I want to disappear. I can't believe this is happening to us. I'm at the end of my rope, and You have to do something quick. Haven't we been through enough?

Even though we struggled a lot during that time and didn't know where the money was coming from to pay the monthly bills, God always provided. We never went without food or shelter. And we never missed a mortgage payment.

On the day that I bought my God-blouse, I had some time to kill as I waited to pick up the children from school. *I'll just browse around the corner boutique. Even if I don't have money, I can still window shop,* I told myself.

I took my time browsing around the store, looking at all the pretty summer clothes on display. I loved the mini-skirts. *I wish I had money to buy something, God.*

I spotted the clearance sale sign in the back of the store and quickly walked over to the clothing rack   I had no intention of buying anything, but the blouse jumped out at me. I fell in love with it. The delicate, soft pink roses on the collar of the blouse looked pretty and would look great with my black pants.

Wow, *it's only ten dollars,* I thought to myself.

I wanted to forget that my husband was out of work and I couldn't afford it.

You don't need a blouse Pat; you have plenty of clothes in your closet, my conscience argued. As I reluctantly placed it back on the rack, I heard that small still voice of God say:

BUY IT AND I WILL PROVIDE.

I pulled out my wallet to see how much money I had in it. I had a ten dollar bill tucked away in the billfold. And in Massachusetts, clothing was tax free. I had exactly the right money to buy that blouse-no more, no less.

God, did I hear you right?

BUY IT AND I WILL PROVIDE.

Is my imagination running wild? If I spend the money on a blouse, where will I get the money to buy milk and bread on my way home?

I wanted to believe it was God, but could I trust myself? In the past, miracles happened when I listened to God. I prayed quietly to myself and listened. My gut was saying - *trust God and buy the blouse.* I decided to buy the blouse.

I picked up the children from school and drove directly home (not saying a word to anyone about my purchase.) I grabbed the mail from the mailbox as I walked in the house, hoping there weren't any bills.

Nothing important, just the usual junk mail, I thought to myself.

What's this? A letter with no return address on it? Who could this be from?

I quickly opened it, eager to see what was inside. My heart skipped a beat when I saw the crisp new ten-dollar bill tucked inside the note card. As I read the simple but profound message written in the card, I started to tremble from head to foot.

Oh my God, I shouted as the tears streamed down my cheeks. *Who sent this to me?* I frantically searched for a name, but there was no name anywhere. Sprawled across the handwritten note was simply,

To Pat,

From the Son of a Carpenter

"Mamma, what's the matter? Why are you crying?" asked my daughter who heard my sobs from the dining room.

"I'm fine, honey. I'm just happy because God loves us so much."

In her sweet little voice she asked, "What did God do to make you cry?"

Filled with awe and gratitude, I couldn't stop laughing and crying at the same time.

God provides, but I didn't expect it so dramatically and so quickly. I still don't know who sent the card and money - and probably never will. The person who sent it listened to the small still voice of God and obeyed. Twenty five years later, I still wear my God-blouse and get compliments. It's always an opportunity to tell the story of God's magnificent love.

Do you believe God guides you and is interested in your everyday life? *I do.*

Wouldn't it be nice to know exactly what to do next? Most of us want a road map, telling us what to do and where to go.

"We expect to be *sure* of God's leading. Being sure eliminates the need for faith and God wants our faith muscles to grow. We don't want to walk by faith; we want certainty! God will not let you be 100% sure. God will guide you, but His guidance is not so explicit or detailed that you don't have to exercise faith in following it." (Basham, 1975.)

Faith is trusting that God will provide and take care of us, no matter what.

"God directs us by dropping his thoughts into the midst of our own, not by thundering in our ears or striking us with heavenly lighting. God guides us through sending subtle impressions. We can then act on faith on those impressions, trusting they're from God." (Basham, 1975.)

I try to listen to my intuition and to the wisdom within. I pay attention to what's going on around me and pray and meditate on a daily basis. I want to be ready when God says to go this way or that way, do this or do that.

I catch myself wanting to know HOW everything is going to work out and I want to know it NOW. My fears come to the surface when I don't have all the answers right at my finger tips. In the past, I have given up following my dreams because fear gripped me in the pit of my stomach, and I became stuck. I didn't know how to take it a step at a time, trusting God would give me what I needed at the right time, not before.

"God Winks" by Squire Rushnell is a book about how God winks at us. Rushnell says, "A God wink is a message of reassurance coming when you most need it; when you are at a crossroads in your life, and when instability is all around you. It might be said, in fact, coincidences are the best way for God to establish a perpetual presence in your life." (Rushnell, Atria 2001)

I call them "GODincidences" and "touches from heaven." God guides me in many ways: through intuition, thoughts and inner wisdom, other people, prayer and meditation and through the bible and spiritual books. God often guides and encourages me through my nightly dreams. Some days I just read or hear something that's exactly what I need to move on. Sometimes, God speaks through synchronicities, putting me in the right place at the right time. God wants to guide us and will use any means to get our attention.

For me, guidance is like dancing with God. He leads; I follow. The word guidance is *God –u and I dance.* When we're both leading, it looks terrible because we're stepping on each other's feet. When He's leading and I'm following, we dance beautifully together. My feet may learn the steps, but it's my spirit that dances.

Will *you* join the dance?

I Am a Woman Giving Birth to Myself

JOURNAL PAGE

What is my experience of God providing for me?

_____

_____

_____

_____

_____

_____

_____

_____

_____

_____

_____

_____

_____

_____

_____

_____

_____

_____

_____

_____

_____

_____

_____

V

Messages
≈ *From Heaven* ≈

Does God Speak to Us Through Songs?

Family and friends filled St Helena's church in the Bronx, New York on a cold and snowy morning January first, 1968. I sat in the front pew anxiously waiting for mom and dad to walk down the aisle as they did twenty five years before. Excitement and anticipation filled the air as we waited for the organist to start playing.

Mom's drinking caused many problems in my parent's relationship and in the family. My parents often fought, and mom talked about divorce when she got drunk. Too many times to count, I cried and begged them not to get a divorce.

Mom found the halls of Alcoholics Anonymous and got sober the year before they celebrated their twenty fifth wedding anniversary. My parents enjoyed that year of her sobriety and looked forward to their second honeymoon in Italy.

They said their final vows to one another and the mass ended. They turned around with big smiles on their faces and started walking back down the aisle.

Mom suddenly collapsed and fell to the floor with a loud bang. At first, I thought she tripped, but then realized she was out cold. The organist stopped playing and people scurried about trying to see what was going on in the front of the church.

My father tried to help her up, but couldn't lift her. Some men rushed forward to help. They carried her to the nearby pew and placed her down. A nurse sitting in the back of the church came forward and administered smelling salts and mouth to mouth resuscitation. Nothing worked as her coloring changed to ash grey.

My heart raced and my hands were sweating as I struggled to hold back the tears. I felt terrified not knowing what was going on. I knelt at the altar, looked up at the cross and prayed.

Please God don't let my mother die. I need her. Where is the ambulance? Why are they taking so long?

I heard the back door of the church open as the fire fighters rushed forward to the front pew to help my mother. I anxiously watched them put the oxygen mask on her face and carry her out on a stretcher to take her to the hospital. I reassured myself, *everything is going to be alright now.*

My father rode in the ambulance and I followed behind in my own car. I grabbed the steering wheel so tight that my hands hurt. I parked the car outside the emergency room entrance and raced in the door.

"Where's my mother?" I screamed to the nurse approaching me.

With that, my father came running toward me hysterical, "Mommy's dead. They couldn't save her."

"No. She's not dead. Where is she? I want to see her."

"Come this way," said the nurse. She led us into a sterile, white-walled room where mom lay motionless on the table.

I sobbed as my father held me in his arms and I said "goodbye" to my mother for the last time. I found out later she died in the church and arrived at the hospital already dead.

We cancelled the reception and luncheon following the mass, as well as their honeymoon to Europe.

My father and I drove home in total silence, both immersed in our own thoughts and loss. Another party was planned in the evening at our home for the friends who didn't come to the church in the day. They arrived with presents in their hands, unaware of what happened at the church that morning. I answered the door as each guest arrived.

"My mom's dead. She died of a heart attack this morning in church."

"Oh my God. I'm so sorry, Pat."

It was such a shock that some people couldn't talk and just wept in my arms. There was nothing anyone could say that would ease the pain. My mother was dead. I needed to be strong for my father because he was falling apart.

My mother died thirty nine years ago when I was twenty years old.

Yet, she stills keeps in contact with me—mostly through songs.

The music played softly in the background as I sat on my living room couch crocheting a baby blanket for my friend Tara. I loved sitting and enjoying the quiet, taking time from my usually busy life. I jumped up and turned up the volume to hear the words better. *"Honey I miss you and I'm being good. An angel came and took her away."* As I sat on the floor and listened, the tears ran down my cheeks and goose bumps spread across my body. My mother's name was Honey.

The song *Honey* by Bobby Goldsboro was written shortly after my mother died thirty nine years ago on New Year's Day. To this day, I still hear the song and it touches me as deeply as it did the first day I heard it. The song describes my mother to a T. I know it's my mother's way of communicating with me and letting me know she's with me and everything is okay. That's just like my mother to have a song written after her.

Sometimes I'm surprised when I hear the song and other times I need to hear it, especially if I'm going through a difficult time in my life. Being twenty years old when my mother died wasn't easy, especially when I got married and started having children. I missed my mother and wanted to talk with her. When I became pregnant with my third child, I prayed for a little girl and often heard the song *Honey* during my pregnancy. I felt comforted knowing mom was with me when I heard the song.

As the nurses wheeled me into the delivery room, after ten hours of labor, I heard *Honey* playing over the loud speaker. I knew at that moment I was having a girl. I cried when I held my daughter Mary for the first time. All the nurses commented what a beautiful head of hair she had. They even put a pink bow in her hair when they brought her to me to be fed. I held her to my heart - my gift from God.

Fast forward ten years. A job opportunity opened up for my

husband and we jumped at it, even though it was in Rhode Island, hundreds of miles away from where we lived. Although we knew it would be difficult leaving our friends and family in Warminster, Pennsylvania, we believed it was God's will and He would provide for us.

My husband started his new job in Rhode Island and couldn't be with us the day we moved. I packed the station wagon so full that I could barely see out of the back window. I tearfully said goodbye to my friends and family. I watched as the mover's carried the last box out of the house and went on their way. The only thing left in the house was the radio on the mantel piece. As I sat on the den floor saying goodbye to the house my children were born in, it finally hit me. We were leaving our family and friends and going to a place where we knew no one. I suddenly felt afraid and anxious, not knowing what the future would bring. I hadn't even seen the house my husband rented for us. I prayed and asked God for strength and courage. As I sat there quietly praying, I heard *Honey* playing on the radio. Filled with gratitude and peace, I thanked God, knowing that everything would work out. There was *Honey* coming to comfort me in my time of need.

Years later, as I began my usual Saturday morning yard sale forays, I longed to feel my mom's presence because I hadn't heard the song on the radio for a long time. I spotted the small mahogany organ as soon as I walked into the yard sale. It brought back memories from my teenage years when mom forced me to take organ lessons. I walked over to the organ to see if I could remember anything, other than *Silent Night*. The wind blew open a music book lying on top of the organ. I looked at the page—a song sheet for the song *Honey* was staring at me. Another touch from heaven exactly when I needed it. I never know where and when mom would show up.

Honey Emails

New Year's Day is the anniversary of my mother's death. It's my ritual to take time for prayer and meditation. I think about what I've accomplished, where I've grown and the lessons I've learned.

Like everyone else, I make resolutions and set goals for the coming year.

When I woke up that New Year's Day 2005, I immediately thought about my mother and how much I missed her. The feelings of loss and sadness surprised me because she had been dead for many years. I asked to feel her love and presence and went about my day. I sat in my cozy den with the fire place blazing and finished *The Secret Lives of Bees* by Sue Monk. My friend Sandra gave it to me as a Christmas gift and I loved reading the story about bees and honey and a girl whose mother died when she was four. In her search to find out about her mother, she found herself and the awareness of the mother within all of us. The story touched my heart as I related to her struggle.

I just finished reading the book and decided to see if my computer worked. My computer needed to be repaired and hadn't worked in over a month.

God, why am I putting it on now? I know it doesn't work. To my surprise, it came right on—no problems. *All these emails, I'll never get through all of them.* I thought. I almost didn't open this particular email because I didn't recognize the name and it looked like just another poem. Something prompted me and I opened it, though. It turned out to be heavenly sent and a gift from my mother on New Year's Day.

YOU REALLY ARE A HONEY

BEE BUSY—DOING WHAT YOU LOVE TO DO

BEE TRUE—TO THE DREAMS GOD HAS GIVEN YOU

BEE SURE—TO TASTE THE SWEETNESS OF EACH DAY

BEE SILLY—GIGGLE LOTS… TAKE OFF AND PLAY

BEE BOLD—ENOUGH TO TRUST YOUR WINGS AND FLY

BEE LIEVE—THE POWER OF PRAYER WILL GET YOU THROUGH

BEE HAPPY—KEEP YOUR OUTLOOK BRIGHT AND HAPPY

BEE YOURSELF

BEE   CAUSE

YOU REALLY ARE A HONEY

(This text was emailed to me and I have been unable to locate its source or determine any copywrite for the material. Any copywrite brought to the author's attention and proven, will be corrected in the next printing of the book and given correct attribution. Please forgive any error of omission.)

God answered my prayer in a strange and mysterious way. He knew I needed to hear from my mother; but I didn't expect it would come through the computer.

Two years later on New Years Day while returning a Christmas gift to the store, I heard the small still voice of God say:

I HAVE A SPECIAL GIFT FOR YOU TODAY. BE OPEN.

God, I love surprises, I wonder what it is? As I walked around the store, I prayed to be led to my gift. But, nothing came to me.

Did I really hear you God? Maybe it was my imagination after all. I was about to leave the store, but decided to take one more look and walked down the baby aisle. I picked up the soft cuddly teddy bear and held it close to my face. When I turned it over, I saw the manufacturer's tag on the back. "Honey" was in big red letters. I smiled and thanked God for my gift. I still squeeze the bear when I'm feeling out of sorts or overwhelmed with life.

Honey at the Restaurant

A new patient of mine shared the same name as a family member of mine. They even shared the same long blonde hair and green eyes. Whenever I looked at her I felt overwhelmed by feelings of sadness. For several years she'd been in and out of treatment centers trying to get sober. I loved her, yet felt powerless to help her stop abusing. Here I was a substance abuse therapist, and I couldn't stop the disease in my own family. I barely managed to get through the day and held back the tears whenever I thought about the situation.

After an emotional day at work, I looked forward to meeting my other son, Tim, for dinner that night. I poured out my heart to Tim as he drove to the restaurant. As we sat down and I tried to decide between chicken fajitas and a burger, I heard the song *Honey* playing on the radio. I looked at Tim and burst into tears. He reached for my hands, held them tightly and waited for the song to end. As he silently looked into my eyes, I felt his compassion and love.

There she was again, coming to me when I needed her the most. I felt her message from heaven that my family member would recover. Several months later, she entered a substance abuse treatment program and has been sober ever since.

Honey in the Consignment Shop

Dad was dying of cancer. I lived out of state and hadn't seen my father for several months. My step mom warned me that he'd lost thirty pounds in a month's time and was very frail and weak. I didn't want to stare when I saw him for the first time. I remembered my dad as strong and active, playing golf everyday before he got sick. I felt helpless watching him suffer and lose his ability to walk and feed himself on his own. I could see in his face how he hated to use the walker to get around.

God, is this going to be the last time I see him before he dies? I wondered. *I want to tell him how much I love him and I'm going to miss him.* When we were alone, I got up the nerve and asked, "Dad, are you afraid?"

"I don't want to talk about it," he answered abruptly.

He wasn't ready to admit he was dying, but I knew he didn't have much time left.

He could no longer stay at home as his illness progressed. While in the hospital, the doctors tried to keep him alive with more operations and procedures. We talked on the phone, but sometimes he was just too weak to talk. I knew in my heart that it was just a matter of time. My step mom Anne couldn't accept he was dying and expressed her hopes for his recovery. Depressed and despondent, dad no longer possessed the will to live and would no longer talk to me when I called on the phone. While the doctors discussed yet another procedure at his bedside, he looked up at my step mom and the doctors and screamed. "Leave me alone, I want to go home."

At that moment my step mom's denial broke and she was finally ready to let him go. A few hours later, he passed away peacefully with her at his side.

I waited anxiously by the phone, pacing back and forth waiting for Anne to call me. When the phone rang that morning, I knew it was the call that I had been dreading. I hardly recognized Anne's voice through the sobs.

"Pat, your dad died fifteen minutes ago." Dead silence that seemed like an eternity.

"I'm so sorry…Are you all right?" I asked

"He suffered so. He's out of pain now."

I hung up the phone and cried as I rocked in the rocking chair by myself. Later, I walked around my house in a daze, not wanting to believe that he was dead. *God, I'm alone now. With both mom and dad dead, I feel like I'm an orphan.* I needed to get some fresh air and clear my head. I took a walk and looked up in the sky and said, *God please allow me to feel my dad's presence.*

I did what I had to do. I called the children and told them their grandfather died. I ordered the flowers and called the airline to make reservations for us to attend the wake and funeral. I dragged myself to the consignment shop to look for a dress to wear for the funeral. I couldn't concentrate and half heartedly looked through the racks of clothing trying to find a dress.

Honey began playing on the radio. I stood frozen in place for a few minutes, then put my face in my hands and sobbed. The owner of the shop walked over to me. I looked up when she asked, "Are you alright? What's wrong?"

"My father just died," I blurted out through sobs and tears. I explained to her about the significance of the song *Honey* that had just played on the radio. She reached out to touch my shoulder, as I took a few deep breaths to calm myself.

Five minutes later, the song *Daddy's Little Girl* came on the radio. My dad often sang that song to me and it always brought tears to my eyes. Everyone cried when he held me in his arms on my wedding day and we danced to *Daddy's Little Girl.*

God answered my prayer—to feel my dad's presence. Hearing the songs only a few hours after he past away was truly amazing. I found a dress or shall I say the dress found me—I certainly wasn't in my right mind.

As I paid and prepared to leave, *You are My Special Angel* began to play on the radio. My grandmother called me "Angel." Within a half hour, I heard three songs that touched my heart; from my mother, father and grandmother. God carried me through and gave me the strength and courage to buy my dress and take care of other mundane tasks getting ready for a funeral, while my heart still felt so raw.

I Am a Woman Giving Birth to Myself

JOURNAL PAGE

Do my deceased loved ones communicate with me and how?

VI

The "Sky God"
Speaks

God, Do We Really Have to Sell Our House?

My husband complained about his sales job for many years. He hated what he was doing. He felt stuck in a dead end job where there was no satisfaction or fulfillment. I could see the toll it was taking on him as his depression worsened. He didn't want to do the things he used to enjoy and watched TV all the time.

Every weekend, he'd spend hours scouring the newspaper looking for jobs, but to no avail. He sent out resumes and had some interviews, but nothing ever panned out. I felt powerless to help, but listened and tried my best to be supportive, encouraging him not to give up. I knew something would come along if he kept trying. I wasn't totally surprised when he asked to speak with me after dinner about something important.

"I'm thinking about going into business for myself," he nervously blurted out.

"Oh. What kind of business?" I asked

God, I know he's going to say a Christian bookstore.

"I want to open a Christian bookstore."

"I knew you were going to say that," I answered.

"How did you know? We've never talked about it before. I've been thinking about this for a long time, but didn't have the guts to bring it up to you. I didn't think you would go for it."

"I don't know how I knew, I just did."

"What do you think?" he asked.

"I'm not sure. I'm not against it, but we don't know anything about running a bookstore. Where would we get the money? Would you quit your job?" There were so many questions and my mind wouldn't shut off.

"I don't know the answers yet, but I'll do some research and see what I can find out," he answered.

"Okay, I'd like to pray about this and make sure it's God's will."

We agreed to pray and discuss it in another week or so. A week later, I could tell by the look in my husband's eyes and the quivering in his voice that he had something to tell me. I waited anxiously until the children were tucked into bed and he was ready to talk. As we sat next to one another on the big sofa, he grabbed my hand and said, "We have to sell our house if we want to go into business." It took me off guard and I gasped.

"What? You must be kidding."

"No, I'm not. I went to the bank to see about a loan. We're not eligible. The only way we can finance a business is to sell our house."

"There must be another way," I said as the tears rolled down my cheeks. The thought of selling our home and moving when I was pregnant with our fourth child seemed out of the question. I loved our home and that was the last thing I wanted to do.

The pain and despair in his eyes prompted me to ask, "Where would we live if we sold our home?"

"We would have to find a nice place to rent," he answered.

I wanted to be open and I desperately wanted my husband to be happy and fulfilled, but I didn't want to move. Every time we broached the subject I kept repeating, "This is such a big step, we have to make sure it's God."

I prayed about it daily, but no answers came until we attended our weekly prayer meeting at the church. After the singing and praise, the church got very quiet as we waited to hear the prophetic word. Directly in front of us sat a man we had never seen before. He spoke loud and clear,

"If you take big steps with me, I will take big steps with you. If you take small steps with me, I will take small steps with you."

My husband looked over at me as the tears streamed down

my cheeks in disbelief. He gently squeezed my hand and smiled at me. We both knew God had spoken and answered our prayers. We couldn't stop talking about it on our ride home from the prayer meeting. Although we weren't ready to speak it aloud yet, we both knew deep down what we needed to do.

The next day my husband called the real estate agent and we put our house up for sale. We didn't know where we would live, but we trusted God would guide us as He promised in the prophecy. We wanted to find a townhouse to rent. I joked with my husband and said, "It wouldn't surprise me if God was building brand new town houses nearby."

The next week as I read the newspaper, savoring my flavorful cup of chai, I spotted the full page ad in the middle section of the paper.

I called out to my husband, "Come quick, look what I found in the newspaper. It looks perfect for us."

GRAND OPENING—TOWNHOUSES FOR RENT OR SALE

We packed the three children in the car and off we went to the neighboring town.

As we drove up the long windy driveway, we couldn't wait to see what the townhouses looked like. Dozens of people walked in and out of the model townhouses.

"How may I help you?" asked the saleswoman who greeted us at the entrance of the model. She smiled as she noticed my obvious big belly and our three young children tagging behind us.

"We're interested in renting a three bedroom townhouse,"my husband answered.

"I'd be glad to show you around. We've already rented several of them today. Aren't they beautiful?" the saleswoman commented.

"Very," I answered. I loved the large rooms and the patio. I imagined our children playing in the small back yard.

"When will they be available to occupy?" I asked

"Some are ready now. We're still building on the other side of the street and they'll be completed in the Spring."

My husband and I walked outside to discuss whether to put a deposit down on the townhouse. Even though we just put our house on the market the week before, we thought it would sell quickly and we needed a place to live when it did sell. The timing seemed perfect and we loved the townhouse. We could afford the monthly payment and it was close to everything. We put down a deposit that day with the understanding that when our house sold, we would move in.

As expected, our house sold quickly and amazingly we got almost to the penny what we needed to open the business. Everything ran on schedule and according to plan. Several months later, we moved into our new townhouse.

Unfortunately, we realized rather quickly that townhouse living was not what we wanted or expected. The constant fighting and yelling of our neighbors on both sides of us made it difficult to sleep at night. The police were constantly being called to break up fights. I jumped up out of bed this one particular night when I heard the sirens and saw the flashing lights outside our bedroom window.

God, what are we going to do? I thought you led us here. This isn't a safe place for the kids. Please show us what to do. We have to get out of here.

"Honey, we can't stay here, I'm afraid something bad will happen. The kids can't even play outside with all the swearing and fighting going on." We complained to the management, but there was nothing they could do about it. We threatened to break the lease if it didn't stop. We thought about buying another house, but we didn't know where the money would come from. All our money went into the business we were in the process of opening.

We prayed and asked God to lead us. We both sensed we were being guided to look for another house to buy. We found an affordable house we liked. It had five bedrooms with a big back yard and a safe neighborhood. We felt strongly God was leading us and He would provide the money somehow.

A friend of ours suggested that my husband apply for a VA loan since he was a veteran and would be eligible. Our friend just bought a house through a VA loan and only needed a small amount of money for a down payment. That sounded like a great idea and my husband called the bank the next day to apply. We received the papers within a few days. We filled out the papers immediately and returned them to the bank. We scheduled an appointment to meet with the manager in two weeks.

"I'm sorry, sir. It's unlikely you'd be eligible for a mortgage with all your money tied up in your new business."

"I know, but I can still apply, right?" my husband answered.

"Yes, you can. I just want to be up front with you about the unlikelihood of it going through."

My husband thanked him and said, "I'll give it a chance."

Our real estate agent knew about our faith and that we were trusting God to get us the house. She tried to be positive, but it was obvious she had her doubts.

She called one day and said, "Pat, I don't think it's a good idea to put all your eggs in one basket. What if this house falls through? What will you do?" Are you sure it's a good idea to give your notice at the townhouse before you know for sure you can get a mortgage?"

"Thank you Darlene for your concern. I know it doesn't look good on paper, but my husband and I are certain it's God's will and it will go through." Sometimes, it's just God's grace that gives you that kind of certainty—a knowing deep within.

We stepped out in faith and gave our notice at the townhouse. We started packing boxes, acting as if all was well. We didn't hear anything for awhile and hoped that was a good sign. With only two weeks left before the closing of the house, we became nervous. The boxes were stacked high in the living room and dining room – we were moving, no matter what.

When I answered the phone, I could hear the hesitation in Darlene's voice that she didn't have good news. I took a deep breath and listened carefully.

"Pat, this is Darlene, I'm sorry but I just got a phone call from the manager of Sovereign bank. Your mortgage wasn't approved. I'm sorry, I know how you were trusting God."

"Is there anything we can do?" I blurted out. "Would you give me the manager's name at the bank? Maybe my husband can call him and explain our situation."

"I'm really not supposed to do this. I could get fired...but, I'll give it to you, if you don't tell anyone where you got it from."

"Thank you, I promise we won't tell."

I immediately called my friend Charlene to pray together on the phone. We asked God for a miracle. I called my husband and gave him the bad news.

"Darlene just called and told me we weren't approved for the mortgage."

"What? That can't be. Can I call someone?"

"Yes, Darlene gave me the manager's name at the bank. It's Mr. Simeone, but don't tell him where you got his name."

My husband called the bank and got directly through to the manager.

"Mr. Simeone, I recently applied for a VA mortgage at your bank. We just got the news that we weren't approved."

"Why are you calling me? What do you want me to do about it?" he answered abruptly.

"I'm just asking to see if there's anything you can do for us. Maybe there's been a mistake."

"I'll check it out and call you back."

"Thank you Mr. Simeone, I appreciate it." A half hour later he called my husband back and said, "I completely agree with this disposition. You weren't approved because your money is tied up in the new business." Silence. For some unknown reason the manager then asked my husband, "What makes you think that this business is going to be successful?"

My husband doesn't even remember what he said, but made up some story of why he thought it would succeed- "It's the only Christian bookstore in the area and I know it's going to be successful."

To my husband's surprise and delight, the manager replied, "Okay, I'll approve it."

Divine intervention. God was true to His promise.

If we took big steps with him, he would take big steps with us.

It was our faith, trust and prayer that moved mountains. We did our part and God did His. I couldn't wait to call Darlene and tell her the good news.

"Darlene, my husband just finished talking to Mr. Simone at the bank and he approved our mortgage."

"Wow. You must know someone *upstairs.* I have a stack of mortgages here in front of me that didn't qualify and they were much better than yours. Can I send them over to you?"

As always, God was glorified and we moved into the house right on schedule.

"The Alleluia Shop"

While praying one day for the name of the store, the "The Alleluia Shop" came into my mind as a good name for a Christian bookstore. A week later, a close friend came to us and said, "I've been praying about a name for the store. How does *The Alleluia Shop* sound to you?" God was moving and we were excited to be part of His plan.

So many of our friends and family members helped us get ready to open the shop. We built bookcases, painted the walls and even put a new floor in. They felt a part of it, like it was their baby too. We advertised the grand opening on the radio and scheduled a famous author, Harold Hill who wrote *How to Live Like a King's Kid* for a book signing. Excitement and nervousness mounted as the big day approached.

The morning of the grand opening my husband woke up deathly ill. What a disappointment for both of us because he had to stay home all day in bed. I called our friends and asked for help. I didn't have a clue what to do and walked around half in a daze with a silly grin on my face. People from all over came for the grand opening and it was a huge success.

There were many challenges we encountered in opening our business. We learned through trial and error and we learned quickly. God provided everything we needed at the exact time we needed it. Our supportive friends often worked at the store so we could have time together as a family. It wasn't just a business, but a ministry where people came to talk and be prayed with.

The Alleluia Shop succeeded for five years. We were the only Christian bookstore in the area that served both the Catholic and Protestant populations. When another Christian bookstore opened down the street, finances became tighter. We tried everything to stay afloat, but we weren't able to make ends meet. Our prayer group and friends prayed for us weekly. They didn't want us to go out of business and helped out however they could.

God often provided money and food through the generosity of others. One day, a young girl, whom we didn't know, walked into the store and handed us a twenty dollar bill for no reason. I came home from a prayer meeting one night and found two crisp hundred dollar bills stuffed in my pocketbook. Friends sent baskets of food with canned goods and a turkey with all the fixings to our home for Thanksgiving. Although we were extremely grateful for all of the love and support bestowed on us, learning to receive was a humbling experience. God was teaching us to trust and depend on Him.

We couldn't afford health insurance and I was eight months pregnant. I wasn't worried because I knew they would send us a hospital bill if we didn't have the money to pay when I was discharged. We trusted God would take care of us and provide. *He did.* Three weeks before my due date, friends came to us and said, "God wants us to pay your hospital bill." Stunned and grateful for their generosity and willingness to listen to God and obey, we received their generous gift. I entered the hospital on my birthday and gave birth to our daughter Mary on October third. Friends paid the hospital bill in full.

Another example of how God provided:

One of our regular customers, Trinia called and asked, "Would you and your husband like to be our guests tonight at our country club?"

"Sure, we'd love to." We hadn't been out to dinner in a long time and it sounded like fun. I knew my husband would say "yes" and we could get a babysitter easily. We didn't know her husband, but that didn't matter.

Our conversation flowed as we got to know one another and ate our dinner. We chatted about the recent mall that just opened up in the state and the new Governor who had just taken office. The men had a lively conversation about the Red Sox who had just won the championship.

Trinia turned to me and quietly said, "Milton and I know things haven't been going too well for you in the business. Is there anything that you need? We'd like to help."

Our mortgage was due in a week and we didn't know where the money would come from. After a couple glasses of wine, my inhibitions were down. I blurted out, "We don't have money to pay our mortgage next month."

"How much is it?" she asked.

"It's $1,000."

"I'll talk to Milton about it tonight."

I didn't know if she really meant it or not, but I knew I would find out soon enough.

A few days later, we received a check for the full amount in the mail.

We hung on for as long as we could and prayed for a miracle. We knew God led us into the business and it was hard accepting that He was now closing the door. We had to accept there was something else for us to do, that our work was done there. And by the grace of God, we moved on with many memories of how God provided so often through the generosity and love of other people.

I Am a Woman Giving Birth to Myself

JOURNAL PAGE

When have I taken a risk that altered the direction of my life?

_____

_____

_____

_____

_____

_____

_____

_____

_____

_____

_____

_____

_____

_____

_____

_____

_____

_____

_____

_____

_____

VII

Divine
⌒ *Connection* ⌒

How to Experience God's Love Through Prayer and Meditation

Draw near to God and He will draw near to you (James 4:5)

Throughout this book, I have shared my personal story. Now I want to move beyond my story alone and help you learn the tools that have made such a powerful impact on my life. In particular, I'd like to share both the power of prayer and specifically how I pray, that it may be of some benefit to you.

The Power that created the universe created you and me. Human beings consist of the same intelligent energy that governs the rest of the earth and the entire universe. This loving energy is available to all of us. We can tap into this force or Power by developing a *relationship* with God through prayer and meditation.

There are as many definitions of prayer as there are people. I don't believe there is a right or wrong way to pray. We must each find what works for us and then do it faithfully. Prayer is a discipline.

Mother Theresa wrote:

"Feel often during the day the need for prayer and pray. Prayer opens the heart, till it is capable of containing God himself. Ask and seek and your heart will be big enough to receive Him as your own."

Billy Graham wrote:

"Prayer is spiritual communication between man and God, a two way relationship in which man should not only talk, but listen to God. Prayer to God is like a child's

conversation with his father. It is natural for a child to ask
his father for the things he needs."

Prayer is the glue that holds my life together. Without prayer
and a personal relationship with God, my life would lack meaning
and purpose. I pray because I want to know and love the Divine
within and experience His unconditional love.

Prayer sustains me on a daily basis. It changes me on the inside,
making me strong, confident and loving. Through prayer, God heals
and transforms me into the woman I am today—A Woman Giving
Birth to Myself. When I'm in the presence of God, I change.

By praying, I stopped looking outside myself for my truth and
started trusting my own experience as sacred. I learned to listen
and trust the wisdom within. I accepted full spiritual responsibility
for my life.

Prayer is making a deliberate conscious contact with God in
word and thought. It brings my mind into alignment with God. I
connect with God within my very own being. When I pray, I experience deep abiding love, healing, peace and serenity. This loving
force or Power is always present.

Plugging into the Power on a daily basis gives me the power to
create what I want in my life and do God's will. Prayer acts just like
electricity. To get light, you need to plug the cord into the outlet
or else you'll be in darkness. When I pray, I tap into my God- given
power which enables me to live a purposeful life. When I don't pray,
my life can easily spin out of control and I become stressed, overwhelmed, tired and irritable.

Taking time to pray daily is like filling up your gas tank with
free gas. You can't go far on empty. Many people live on their own
power and don't ask for help. No wonder there's so much suffer-
ing, depression, isolation, suicide, fear, hatred and unhappiness;
people don't pray enough and open themselves up to the benefits
of prayer.

If you only knew how prayer could change you and give you
the peace you desire, you would be racing to start a prayer life. It's
God's desire to communicate with you and answer your prayers.
He wants to guide you and give you what you need and desire. He

wants you to depend on Him, trust Him and love Him. An important part of prayer is learning to listen.

I need to be still and quiet to hear God's whisper in my ear. I hear God in the stillness of my soul. Silence is how we come to know God intimately.

You may have a hard time hearing God's voice or feeling His presence. You may not know that He really loves you and wants to communicate with you. Why can't you hear Him? It may be that you are harboring resentment or unforgiveness in your heart. You may be unwilling to let go of judgments, pride, fear, stubbornness or control. You must be willing to change if you want to hear God and receive all that He wants to give you.

REASONS WHY YOU DON'T PLUG INTO THE POWER AND ASK FOR HELP:

1. Do you think you should do it on your own and you're not supposed to ask?

I should know what to do. God's not interested in the daily events of my life. I don't want to bother Him for the small things.

2. Does pride keep you from plugging into the Power and asking for help?

Thank you very much, but I can handle this by myself. I don't need help.

3. Is it your fear?

What will be asked of me if I pray?

4. Do you feel unworthy, ashamed or undeserving?

I don't deserve to ask for help. God has more important things to do than to listen to me.

5. Are you unable to forgive yourself for past failures and mistakes?

God won't forgive me for my past, so I can't ask for anything.

6. Are you angry at God for something that happened in the past? Losing a loved one, a divorce, abusive childhood or losing a job?

These self-defeating thoughts and beliefs will block you from experiencing God's loving presence and guidance. God wants you to ask and believe He will answer in His way and His time. God's timing is perfect. He may not answer the way you would like Him to, but He always answers prayer. It's important to understand that it's not God who goes away and disconnects; we disconnect from God and walk away from Him.

Sometimes God has to work hard at getting your attention, perhaps allowing trials or stumbling blocks in order to get you back on track. Just like a loving father who wants to give everything He can to his children, our Creator desires to pour out His love and blessings on you, if you let Him. To connect with God, you need to *show up.*

Many people have commented about my strong faith and how inspired they are by it. It's why I've written this book. By sharing my faith and prayer with you and how it works for me, my hope and intention is that your faith will grow and you will know that God wants to give you that same faith. I see myself as a woman who has a lot of faith. I trust that when I ask for something, God always answers, but it may not be in the way or timing that I want.

Dr. Norman Vincent Peale, in a booklet entitled *Courage* writes, "One of the most powerful traits in human nature is that when you maintain a mental attitude of trust and faith-when you hope, dream, believe, pray and work toward God's assurance- you will create conditions in which every good thing can come to you. Fill your mind with the positive power of spiritual expectancy, and God and His good will come into your life."

My faith has grown and been strengthened because of a daily prayer life. Each day I make a commitment to come to God, in prayer and thanksgiving. There is an attitude of gratitude, always grateful for the blessings and help He bestows on me.

For me, Prayer is:

- Talking

- Listening

- Meditating

✛ Reflection

✛ Asking

✛ Interceding for others

✛ Giving praise and thanks

✛ Expressing thoughts and emotions

✛ Obeying

✛ Seeking forgiveness for myself and forgiving others

✛ Comforting

✛ Healing

✛ Letting go of problems and worries

✛ Seeking God's will and guidance

How do I know who God is unless I spend time with him? My desire is to know God and be more like Him. Just like any human relationship, we need to spend time getting to know one another in order to grow. It's the same with God.

I've been blessed and graced with a daily prayer time for over thirty years. If I wake up in the morning and feel stressed or rushed, I know that once I sit and pray, my peace returns. I still have the same problems to deal with, but I'm able to turn them over and ask for help. Being human, I may take back my problems, thinking I can handle them on my own. I pray throughout the day, asking for help, guidance and direction.

When I started my prayer life thirty two years ago, ten minutes seemed like a long time, but I kept *showing up* each morning. I had great difficulty shutting my mind off and being quiet. I sometimes still do. It's important to find a place that you can pray and be alone. You can make a little altar with a candle, flower, bible, something that speaks to you, prayer book, spiritual book or rock. I've used the dining room table for my altar when I didn't have a special room to go to. When I was done, I put my special altar pieces in a basket for the next day.

Prayer is a discipline and takes a commitment to yourself and

God. It's important when you start a daily prayer time to pray at the same time each day so it becomes a habit. Of course, there will be times when you cannot pray at that time and that's fine. You can do it another time of the day. Some people pray in the morning, others at night. It's finding what works for you and sticking to it.

How I pray:

⊹ I immediately get on my knees when I get out of bed and say the serenity prayer.

God grant me the serenity to accept the things I cannot change, courage to change the things I can and the wisdom to know the difference.

I cannot change other people, places or things. I can only change myself and that's a big enough job. Letting go and letting God is a conscious choice I make every day. I'm in trouble when I play God and think I know what's best for someone else's life or what they should do. I'm learning and practicing getting out of the driver's seat, avoiding responsibility for everyone and everything around me.

⊹ I pray my intention for the day. My intention is to be peaceful, loving and kind. My intentions may change depending on what I need for the day.

⊹ When I'm ready to sit for my prayer time, I light a candle and greet God

Thank you for bringing me into your presence.

⊹ I close my eyes and start with deep breathing, quieting my mind, letting go of any tension and problems. I breathe in God's love and on the out breath, I breathe out tension and fear. I do this until I feel peaceful and calm. If my mind is racing, it may take awhile to quiet down and become still.

⊹ I intercede for family, friends and those in need.

⊹ I meditate and repeat slowly, "Everything I need is streaming toward me, I open my hands and receive."

All the love I need...All the wisdom I need...All the money I need…All the patience I need…All the friends I need…I put in whatever I need at that moment.

❖ I write in my journal. Journaling my thoughts and feelings is an important part of my prayer. If it's a beautiful day, I thank Him for the sunshine, the breeze and the birds chirping. I think about the day before and thank Him for whatever happened, what I learned or how He helped me with a problem or decision I had to make. If I'm angry, upset or struggling with something, I may write for two pages or more. Other times it's just a paragraph. God knows what's in my heart and I need be honest with all of my feelings. Journaling is a great tool because you can look back over it and see how prayer was answered and how you've changed. I've heard others say "I'm not a writer." You don't have to be. This is for you and no one else is going to read it.

❖ I look over my "Picture Book" with my intentions and dreams in it. It's a small photo album that I put together that has quotes, pictures and scriptures that have meaning to me. I SEE myself as successful, at a book signing for my book, on TV talking about my book and making money to buy my house on the water.

❖ When I'm struggling or questioning my abilities, I read my picture book and find a tremendous amount of energy and power in it.

❖ I pray with *angel messenger cards.* I randomly pick two cards each day. Each card has a different message. It may be Love, faith or inspiration and a host of other messages. God speaks to me through the angels. (Angelic messenger cards, Young-Sowers, Still Point)

❖ I have spiritual books available and read when I'm led.

❖ When I have a dream that's significant, I write it out and ask for God's wisdom. Paying attention to my dreams is a way that God guides and comforts me.

❖ Affirmations are an integral part of my prayer life. An affirmation is what I say to myself to change the negative messages/beliefs about myself, others or my life. My first affirmation was "I like and approve of the person I'm becoming." I repeated this affirmation to myself all through the day until I believed it and it was etched in my consciousness.

✝ I allow the spirit to lead and guide me during my prayer. I may not do everything or follow the exact same format in the same way every day.

I end my prayer with thanksgiving, trusting God that I'm exactly where I need to be and that all my needs are being taken care of.

All throughout the day, I pray my mantra, "My intention is to be peaceful," especially when I notice I'm rushing, feeling judgemental, or out of sorts in some way. While writing this chapter on prayer, God showed me where I needed to change and I'd like to share it with you.

My mind was like a blender and wouldn't shut off. I kept obsessing about how rudely a co-worker treated me. I couldn't wait to get home and tell my best friend what happened. I needed to tell someone. As I pulled into my driveway, I heard God say,

THERE COMES A TIME WHEN OLD BEHAVIORS DON'T WORK ANYMORE. IF YOU WANT TO BE MY INSTRUMENT, YOU HAVE TO STOP COMPLAINING AND TALKING ABOUT OTHERS. I WANT YOU TO PRAY FOR HER INSTEAD OF GOSSIPING ABOUT HER. YOU WOULDN'T LIKE IT IF PEOPLE WERE TALKING ABOUT YOU BEHIND YOUR BACK.

I got the message loud and clear and didn't call my girlfriend to complain. I change in the presence of God.

Some benefits of Prayer and what it can do for you:

1. Without prayer, you only see the visible. With prayer, God shows you the hidden aspects of life.

2. Prayer quiets your fears and calms your nerves.

3. Prayer allows you to let go of burdens and give them to God.

4. Prayer upholds others who are in need.

5. Prayer can provide an experience of love, joy, hope, peace of mind and healing.

6. Prayer can help you grow in self confidence and trust.

7. Prayer opens your heart to others and you become less judgmental.

8. Prayer provides guidance for making daily decisions and solving problems.

Angelic Messenger cards by Young-Sowers offer spiritual seekers a unique and effective tool for developing a direct and meaningful relationship with the Divine through the messages of angelic teachers. The cards act as a living prayer to help us resolve problems, develop inner trust, affirm ourselves and renew and awaken the spiritual energy of love. The cards are a divinely inspired tool for self discovery. We are being called to live with greater awareness of our own spiritual natures as well as our interrelationships with God and all other living things. Angels are actual energy beings or beings of light that are ever-present in our lives.

I Am a Woman Giving Birth to Myself

JOURNAL PAGE

How do I connect with the spiritual power within?

_____

_____

_____

_____

_____

_____

_____

_____

_____

_____

_____

_____

_____

_____

_____

_____

_____

_____

_____

_____

VIII

Slowliness is
⁓ Godliness ⁓

God Speaks Through Symbols

God has been speaking to me about turtles and I'm seeing them all over the place.

Slow and steady, the turtle knows when to move and when to stay still and rest. Through turtles God teaches me about patience and Godliness.

Turtles go within for answers because they know the truth is within. As the turtle knows when to go in, I'm learning to go inside and trust myself, my intuition and my gut. When I go inside, I ask myself "What am I feeling and thinking?" I sometimes need to change my *stinking thinking*. It's so easy to take things personally or jump to conclusions and be negative. When I stick my head out, like the turtle, I ask myself, "What action do I need to take?" It may be that I need to speak up, set a boundary, say "no," forgive someone or let go of a resentment.

While leading a women's spirituality retreat in June of 2005, I shared what God teaches me through the turtle. The next morning, as I looked out my bedroom window, I spotted a huge slow moving turtle walking across the parking lot. I had no idea what a turtle was doing in the parking lot, other than a sign from God that He was with me.

Why is the turtle so powerful a symbol for me?

Most of my life, I've acted just the opposite and never rested or went within for my answers. I constantly raced around, going from one thing to another. Rushing was my addiction. If I rushed and stayed busy, I didn't have time to feel my feelings and go within. It gave me energy when I rushed. I felt powerful when I multi-tasked and felt in control. Just like the alcoholic who uses alcohol to medicate painful feelings, I used rushing to medicate painful feelings from my childhood. I always pushed myself to do more and be more. I never felt good enough and didn't know how to relax.

A friend told me that rushing was abusive and a death wish. It's a death wish because when I rush all the time, I disconnect from myself and from the divine energy of God within. When I rush, I'm not respecting myself or the God within.

God guides through dreams

For weeks, I kept dreaming about going on a vacation and throwing things together in my suitcase at the last minute. In my dreams, I frantically raced around the house trying not to forget anything. My suitcase overflowed with everything I wanted to bring: my hair dryer, my bathing suit, my jacket and of course my self-help books that I wanted to read. I felt panicked, thinking I'd miss the plane if I didn't rush fast enough. God will often send me a dream over and over again until I get the message. I felt frustrated because I knew I wasn't getting the message.

Later that day, I finally got it. God showed me through working with the dream that I've rushed all my life. I had to get things done quickly and I never took my time with anything.

God, where and how did this start? I don't like feeling like this anymore.

God showed me that it started when I was seven years old growing up in my alcoholic home. I never knew if promises were going to be kept because of the drinking. I didn't know if my mom would be there when I got home from school or if she would be drunk. She would often take off for days and nobody knew where she was. It was scary being a little girl and not knowing if my mother was dead or alive when she didn't come home. I never heard the phrase "Take your time" growing up. It was always "Hurry up." Every morning before going to school, my mother would be yelling. "Hurry up or you'll miss the bus."

Rushing became a way of life for me. Although on the outside I may have looked peaceful, there was an "inner rushing" that was pervasive and intense. I had the image of myself as a horse always ready to take off at the gate.

If I wanted peace in my life, I had to change. It only takes one person to change your life—you. I had to slow down, be conscious and learn to live in the moment. I asked God for the grace to slow down and relax. With this new awareness of my rushing and the damage it was doing to me, I started to observe the many areas in my life that I rushed. I walked fast, I drove fast, I ate fast. I even talked fast and sometimes finished others sentences for them.

I recently drove my son to the airport and gave myself plenty of time to get there. We were half way there when he looked over at me and said, "Mom, why are you driving so slow?"

"I'm practicing being in the moment and not rushing," I said.

"You don't need to practice when I'm in the car," he answered with a grin.

Another time, as I drove to Newport on a beautiful sunny day, I drove slowly and stayed in the right hand lane. I kept repeating to myself with my hands on the steering wheel "driving, driving" to practice being in the moment. It took effort and determination to be present as I watched the cars go speeding by me.

I love it when I'm able to just let the day happen with no plans and no place to go. I call it my Bermudiana days. Even if it's not a whole day, a few hours work well. I felt peaceful and alive as I strolled around Newport going in and out of the beautiful shops. I felt the presence of God, grateful to be alive. I've learned to enjoy my own company because I know the most important relationship I have is with myself. This is truly a gift because I didn't always know this.

I found a lovely shop that sold candles, jewelry, gifts and books. I walked over to the book section and randomly picked a book from the shelf and opened a page. My eyes immediately fell to the sentence that read, "Coping with speed has become the heroic journey that consumes the lifetime of the common man and woman. It is our greatest killer. Rushing puts you into adrenaline overload and drenches the body in epinephrine, a hormone stimulated by stress, anger or fear." (Seven Whispers, Baldwin 2002.) This was no coincidence, but a GODincidence. God led me to open the book and read about rushing. I bought the book and spent the rest of the afternoon reading it. It confirmed what God was teaching me about the pace of my life. *Slowliness is Godliness.*

I practice moving slowly on a daily basis, especially at work where it's fast paced and there's so much to do. My intention each day is to be peaceful. I repeat it all during the day, particularly when I'm tempted to rush. I know that I am responsible for the peace and pace I bring to each moment.

When I revert to old rushing behaviors, I remind myself that rushing is abusive and that slows me right down.

My co-worker remarked one day, "Pat, I always know it's you coming down the hall by your meditative walk."

It would surprise her to know what I use to be like, racing around frantically.

I received this prayer on a retreat that I attended five years ago:

May the God of the present moment be with me, slowing me down, revealing to me the sacred gift hidden in each moment of my day. May I develop a reflective heart, able to be present to life, a heart that can take time to move beyond the visible to touch the precious mystery of life and living.

I Am a Woman Giving Birth to Myself

JOURNAL PAGE

In what ways do I avoid going within? How can I support
myself to "go slowly" and turn inwards?

IX

God is My
Travel Agent

A Calling to Bermuda: God Gives Me What I Need

God, are you calling me to Bermuda? Where will I get the money?
Going on a vacation by myself lingered in my mind for a long time, but I never said a word about it to anyone. To even think about going on a vacation alone surprised me because I couldn't even go to a restaurant alone, never mind travel out of the country. I thought people would feel sorry for me sitting alone in a restaurant and would think I didn't have any friends.

If I'm thinking about going on a vacation by myself, I better see if I can go to a restaurant alone, I thought to myself.

I felt awkward the first time I went to lunch by myself to a nice restaurant. I brought a book with me so it wasn't so uncomfortable. As I sat there with my book in hand, waiting for my food to be served, I reassured myself, *You're a big girl now... you can do this... nobody is even looking at you.*

I have to admit, it felt good sitting there and not worrying about what others were thinking of me.

The gnawing feeling in my gut continued to urge me to go on a vacation by myself. Memories of Bermuda danced in my head as I recalled going there for college week thirty years ago. The deep crystal clear turquoise water took my breath away and walking the pink sandy beaches made me want to set up camp and stay there.

With the stress of my husband being unemployed and my own personal problems that I was working through, my body screamed out for attention. I experienced one sleepless night after another, and constant tension headaches during the day. I desperately need- ed peace and tranquility. I felt headed for a nervous breakdown and knew I needed to just do something for myself, away from my family responsibilities.

God speaks to me through my dreams and several times a week during that time, I dreamt about going to Bermuda. I pay attention when I have recurring dreams because God uses them to get my attention.

Where are these dreams coming from God?

Listening to my dreams, as a spiritual practice, has been a great tool for guidance and inspiration. Working with dreams can be a vehicle for self discovery; dreams help me understand where I am and where I'm going.

Okay, God, I'll go to a travel agency and at least check it out.

I jumped in my yellow VW and off I went.

"I'd like to get some information about Bermuda," I asked the salesperson.

"Would you please show me some brochures? I want a safe place for a woman to travel alone."

"Yes, Bermuda is the place to go," she answered. "In fact, we have some great deals that I would be glad to show you. I've trav- eled there myself several times and it's safe. I have the perfect hotel for you."

I instantly fell in love with Angel's Grotto. The picture on the brochure said it all—overlooking a pristine stretch of pink sand and turquoise ocean. It looked like the perfect get away.

I'll never be able to afford this. What am I doing God? I haven't even told my husband about it. He's going to think I'm out of my mind, especially since his unemployment runs out and he doesn't have a job yet.

I reluctantly asked, "What does this all cost?"

"Only $1,200, everything included. You can't beat a price like that. Shall I book it?"

"Well, yes," I stammered. "But I have to check with my husband first and see if he's okay with it. I'll call you tomorrow."

It seemed like a good deal, but I didn't have $1200. I didn't even have $100.

As I began to mull it over, the guilt set in and my inner critic attacked relentlessly.

Who do you think you are even thinking about going away? You're selfish and self- centered. You don't deserve this. You're only thinking about yourself.

I prayed and asked God to guide me. I asked Him to shut the door if this wasn't His will and open it if it was. Slowly and deliberately, I changed my thinking.

I am deserving and there's nothing to be guilty about. God is the source of everything and will provide.

"Honey, I need to talk to you about something important."

My husband placed his newspaper down on the table and looked up from over his glasses. My tone must have been nervous, because he looked alarmed himself.

"I'm thinking about going to Bermuda on vacation - by myself."

"Oh!"

He could see the pain in my eyes and knew how I struggled in my personal life. I had recently started therapy to deal with memories of clergy sexual abuse when I was twelve years old. I could no longer hide the unrest and turmoil.

I told him about my trip to the travel agency and how much it cost.

"Where are you going to get the money?" he asked.

"I'm praying in the money."

"What does that mean?"

"If God wants me to go, He will open the door and provide the money and if not, I won't go." He sat there quietly for awhile thinking and then with some amusement in his voice said, "Go for it."

My husband's support helped me move forward and trust God would provide—if it was His will.

I prayed, waited and watched the money come in. I jumped at it when I received a $50 check from the telephone company inviting me to change carriers.

This must be you God, but there's a lot more I need.

I put an ad in the newspaper for a white fur coat I no longer wore. I only received one phone call inquiring about the coat. When she came and tried it on, she thought it was a bargain for $50.

God, I have nothing else to sell. If you want me to go, I need more money.

A few weeks later, I ran into a neighbor while taking a walk. It surprised the heck out of me when she asked, "Pat, do you know of anyone who can help me with my ninety year old mother who just came home from the hospital? I don't want her to be alone at night. I'm with her in the day and will prepare her evening meal."

"What exactly does the person need to do?" I asked.

"I need someone to come over at five o'clock and sit with her while she has her dinner. They would help her to bed right after supper, and stay with her four hours a night during the week."

"I'm interested." I thought I would jump out of my skin with excitement.

"I can pay ten bucks an hour. Does that work for you?"

"Yes, I'd be glad to help your mother. When do I start?"

"Next week would be great."

The money I made quickly added up and I achieved my $1,200 goal in no time.

God opened the door and provided all the money I needed to go to Bermuda. I marked off the days on my calendar, anticipating the warm breeze and hot sun. I found it hard to concentrate on work, as my mind kept returning to Bermuda's warming lure. At the same time, along with the excitement and anticipation came fear.

I can't believe I'm traveling out of the country all by myself. What if I miss my plane or lose my luggage? What if I get lost? What if I get lonely? I've never done anything like this in my whole life—what might happen to me?

I kept reassuring myself that I would be okay and that God would take care of me.

Since God opened the door and provided the money, I felt sure He would bless me with beautiful weather and a peaceful trip. Just what the doctor ordered.

When the big day finally arrived, I ran around in a frenzy checking my suitcase to make sure I didn't forget anything. My husband drove me to the airport, hugged me goodbye and said, "Don't forget to call me when you get there. You know how I worry."

"Don't worry. I'll call you as soon as I get to the hotel."

"Okay, and have a safe trip."

"Remember, Mary has a birthday party on Saturday and you have to drive her there."

"Yes, dear."

I sat next to a friendly lady on the plane. We chatted the whole time, which made the ride fly by. It was her first trip to Bermuda and she wanted to know all about the island.

As I got off the airplane with my big brimmed straw hat, my new khaki pants (that I purchased with my mom-sitting money) and a big smile on my face, I was greeted with big black clouds hovering above and a chill in the air. Within minutes, the sky opened up and down came the pouring rain. I overheard someone say that a cold front from the US had just come into Bermuda—cold and rainy weather forecast for the next few days.

I must not he hearing right, I'm sure it will pass through quickly and the sun will come out tomorrow. I'm trusting you God, I muttered under my breath.

I shall never forget the ride from the airport to Angel's Grotto. I held my breath and closed my eyes as the taxi driver whizzed around the narrow streets beeping and waving to the other taxi cab drivers coming toward us. It seemed like everyone knew one another. Driving on the opposite side of the street took time getting use to. Looking in his rear view mirror, he could tell by the look on my face that I was nervous. He tried to be friendly.

"Lady, is this your first time in Bermuda?" he asked politely.

"It's my second. What has the weather been like here?"

"It's been beautiful up until today. You know that a cold front from the U.S. just came in?"

"I just heard. I don't expect it to last too long," I said enthusiastically.

"There it is, Angel's Grotto, right up ahead." I couldn't wait to see it and strained my neck trying to get a glimpse. I thanked him for the ride and gave him a generous tip. As quickly as I could, I gathered my bags and shut the door, running toward the beautiful hotel.

As I settled into my room, I thought that the brochure didn't even come close to the natural beauty of this haven. Clearly, I'd made the right decision to come here. I looked out of my living room picture window at the beach and listened to the ocean waves crashing over the rocks—music to my ears.

Thank you God, I know this is going to be a magnificent week... and the sun will come out.

I woke up bright and early the next day. The rain had finally stopped, but no sunshine yet. Well, soon, I knew the sun would shine. I couldn't wait to rent a moped and tour the island remembering how it felt with the wind blowing on my face those thirty years ago. Riding a moped in Bermuda, at seventeen years old seemed easy. I told myself it would come back to me, just like riding a bike. I called the moped shop the next day and asked if they would deliver a moped to the hotel. It didn't take them long to arrive at my doorstep.

When the man arrived with my moped, he looked me over and asked doubtfully,

"Lady, have you ever ridden a moped before?"

"Sure, when I came here thirty years ago." I smugly replied.

He smiled and said, "Let's see what you remember." He showed me the basics in the parking lot—how to turn, stop, speed up and how to turn it off. It's always a sign that I'm nervous when my hands sweat—and they were sweating profusely. I tried to act confident, but he could see the panic in my eyes.

"Are you sure you're okay? I can stay while you practice in the parking lot."

"I'd love your help," I answered. He patiently watched me as I tried to maneuver the bike around. The bike jerked when I stopped and I almost went into the wall. I kept practicing going around and around until I felt confident and ready to ride on my own.

"If you have any problems, call me for help." I thanked him as he opened the door of his truck and waved and drove off.

Pat, you can do this. Just take your time, don't get nervous. You did it when you were seventeen; you can do it now.

I placed the helmet gently on my head, started up the bike and began my tour of the island. I concentrated on staying on the opposite side of the street, knowing it would be easy to forget and end up in the wrong lane. Smooth sailing until I hit the traffic in downtown Bermuda. Well, I didn't literally hit it!

Oh my God, I'm having a panic attack. I can't breathe.

I could hardly see through the tears burning my eyes. My heart pounded a mile a minute and my hands clutched tightly on the gears.

I need help God or I'm going to get myself killed. What the hell am I doing in the middle of the traffic at lunch hour?

I managed to get the moped to the side of the street and breathed a sigh of relief. I had to calm myself down and pull myself together. God sent me an angel. A policeman sitting on the side of the street saw how pale I was, all the color drained from my face.

"Do you need help?" he asked.

I blurted out, "Please help me get out of this traffic before I cause an accident."

He smiled and motioned me to follow him. He stayed with me for quite awhile until I felt comfortable on the moped and in traffic. *I just needed a little practice,* I told myself. I felt proud of myself that I made it home safely and in one piece.

Day two. The pouring rain and threatening black skies kept me inside all day. I made the best of it and cuddled up in front of the window, leisurely reading my Danielle Steel novel, sipping a hot flavorful mug of chai. As I listened to the weather station on the radio every hour on the hour, my enthusiasm faltered.

God, why did you bring me to this beautiful paradise only to wilt in the rain and stormy weather? I don't understand. Please help me to trust you.

Day three. The sun peeked through the clouds. Finally, the weather appeared to be turning. With newfound confidence in my moped skills and my trusty map in my pocket, I jumped on my moped and began anew to tour the island. *Yes I can do this, smooth sailing, I knew I would remember.*

Then, without any warning, my bike stalled on the side of the road. Panic struck.

What am I going to do now? I turned the key slowly to see if I could get it started. The bike just wouldn't start no matter what I did. I looked around the desolate stretch of road- no one in sight to ask for help. I sat there for awhile completely paralyzed and void of any intelligible thought. Fear gripped me in the pit of my stomach as the sweat poured down my forehead.

You should never have come here alone. What if someone robs you? Or kidnaps you? People take advantage of stranded women all the time. How could you be so stupid as to put yourself in this situation.

As I sat there wondering what to do next, a man drove by on his moped and saw me sitting there. God sent another angel to help.

"What's wrong?"

"My moped stalled and I can't get it started," I replied.

"Let me see what I can do." In a second he came up with the diagnosis. "Your gas tank is empty."

"Gas tank empty?" I hadn't even asked the man who delivered the moped where the gas tank was. I blushed as I tried to make excuses for my stupidity.

"I didn't think the gas would run out. Why didn't they show me where the gas tank was in the first place?" I blurted out. I had to blame someone.

"There's a gas station right up the street. I'll go and get you some gas."

As I sat there waiting for the gas, I thanked God for sending me this nice, helpful Bermudian rather than the Boston Strangler. When he returned, I paid him for the gas, thanked him profusely for his help and resumed my island tour.

I looked forward to riding to St. George for lunch. Even though it was on the other side of the island, it would be worth the trip. I remembered the quaint little shops and eating in the restaurant that served rich chocolate cake that melted in my mouth.

As I drove into St. George, all I could see were the majestic cruise ships lined up along the ocean front. People were standing on the decks watching and waving to those passing by. I leisurely strolled around town enjoying the sights and taking my time to browse in the novelty shops. I stopped to watch a man making glass jewelry. I finally felt that vacation sense of freedom, as I strolled along the streets browsing in shops.

I have all the time in the world. For once, I have no agenda.

I found a cozy restaurant tucked away behind the famous St. George cathedral. Two men played chess in a corner and there was a sense of liveliness in the conversation at the other two tables. *This is what I call a vacation God, thank you.*

I expected my trip back to be uneventful as I strapped on my helmet and started up my moped. The air felt different and it seemed a little darker. I looked up in the sky and knew rain was only minutes away.

God, what's going on? Where's the sun? I don't even have a rain-coat with me.

As I raced against time to get back to Angels Grotto, black ominous clouds threatened from above and the cold wind chilled my weary bones.

I have to get back on my own, no matter what. Maybe I can make it before it gets really bad.

Within minutes, the sky opened up and the rain poured down. I could hardly see as the hail and ice balls hit my face. As each car sped by, water splashed my feet, legs, arms and even my head. Between my tears and the pouring rain, I could hardly see in front of me. I held on for dear life. I had to keep going, no matter what. My body trembled with fear and I felt my heart pound inside my chest.

God help. I'm scared to death and my life is in danger.

Up ahead, as I squinted to see, I spotted a covered shelter for people waiting for buses.

If I can reach that shelter, I can get out of the rain and be safe until it passes. Keep going Pat. You're gonna make it. Just keep moving and you'll be safe.

As I approached the shelter, I could see it was empty. I turned off my moped, threw it on the ground and screamed at God at the top of my lungs.

F U God

I felt the anger rise up from a place deep within me. I didn't get angry at God—ever. What was going on with me? I have no idea how long I sat on the ground sobbing uncontrollably, but it seemed like time had stopped. I realized that all my life I held in my anger and I couldn't hold it in any longer. Once it started, it wouldn't let up until it ran its course. After this outburst and release of anger, I calmed down and felt better. Although totally spent and exhausted, I knew deep down that something had shifted inside of me. The weather had shifted as well.

The rain had stopped and I couldn't wait to get back to the hotel. Drenched and cold, I peeled off my clothes layer by layer, then soaked in a hot tub for over an hour, adding hot water as it cooled. As soon as my head hit the pillow that evening, I was out and I slept like a baby.

When I woke up the next morning, the sun shone brightly through my window. I listened to the bird's song and felt renewed. I felt transformed, healed and loved. Looking out my window at the pale blue, clear sky, I felt peaceful, serene and grateful as if enveloped in God's loving presence.

God, something feels different inside, what happened yesterday? I feel lighter and more alive. Where did all that anger come from? I'm sorry God for blaming you and saying what I did.

Sitting in prayer and meditating the next day, I sensed the beginning of getting in touch with a well of deep unresolved anger from my childhood. I didn't know how much anger I had inside of me until my moped incident. I could no longer keep the lid on my anger because it was destroying me. I thought about the headaches and not sleeping—they were probably a result of my unresolved anger and holding things in.

I think God, in His ultimate wisdom, allowed this to happen so I could begin to release the anger from the sexual abuse that I'd buried for years. He knew it would take a lot for me to get angry —alone in Bermuda on a moped during a hail storm did it. Clearly, the release was more important to my well being than having beautiful weather. Yes, I was angry and wanted to blame God for the bad weather, and for my fears of getting electrocuted or having an accident on the moped.

God had thrown His thunderbolts and created the perfect circumstances to free and heal me. I thought I was going to Bermuda to rest and relax in the sunshine. God had other plans, better plans. He knew exactly what I needed.

I Am a Woman Giving Birth to Myself

JOURNAL PAGE

Have I ever been struck by God's thunderbolts?
How did it feel? What did I learn from it?

_____

_____

_____

_____

_____

_____

_____

_____

_____

_____

_____

_____

_____

_____

_____

_____

_____

_____

_____

_____

X

God's Divine
Employment Agency
How to Find a Job the God Way

God led me and opened the doors for my last three jobs. When my children were growing up I stayed home so I didn't have a skill to turn to when they started school.

It was my turn now—I wanted to do something for myself, but I didn't know what it was. I thought about going back to school, but struggled with doubts and fears, especially after being out of school for twenty six years.

God, what would I be good at? I like helping people and I'm a good listener. People have always been drawn to me and tell me they trust me. I'd really like to be a substance abuse therapist and get paid for what I do best.

I prayed about it for awhile before making up my mind. I decided to sign up for an Alcohol and Drug class at the local community college. What a challenge—I didn't like school and studying during high school. I enjoyed football games, cheerleading and weekly dances.

My oldest son Brian and I started Community College of RI together. I felt proud of him as we walked up the stairs to the huge brick building we were about to enter.

God, where did the time go to? I remember walking him to school on his first day of kindergarten. I looked up at him and smiled.

We walked into the building, ready to part ways. He could see the fear all over my face and gently said, "Mom, you're going to be fine, relax. I'll meet you here after classes," and off he went.

I walked around looking for my classroom in a daze. As I looked around, I realized I must have been the oldest student there. It seemed to me that all the other students knew each other, as they laughed and joked around together in the halls.

When I found the classroom and peeked in, I felt so nervous that I fantasized about turning around and running straight home. *What am I doing going back to school at my age?* I asked myself. *Everyone else is under twenty. I don't fit in at all. God, I need your help.* I heard the small still voice of God say:

Pat, I'm with you. Don't be afraid. This is my will and I will give you what you need. Trust me.

Okay God, as I held my breath and walked in. I quickly found a seat in the back of the room hoping no one would notice me back there. As I sat down, the young man sitting next to me said, "Hi, I'm Bill, what's your name?"

"Pat."

"You look nervous. Is this your first day of college?"

I had to hold back my laughter. I didn't realize it was so obvious.

"Yes, I've been out of school for twenty six years." I replied.

"Good for you. My mom went back to school a few years ago and she did great. I'm sure you'll do great too." I took a deep breath and started to relax, grateful to Bill for putting me more at ease.

It took my brain some time to get acclimated to studying. I worked hard in the class and wanted to get all A's to prove to myself that I wasn't stupid. Halfway through the class, I approached my teacher and asked, "Do you know of any substance abuse agencies that might be hiring? I'd like to work in the substance abuse field to make sure I'm on the right track."

"I don't know if they're hiring, but you can give Lorraine Costa a call at Alcohol Drugs and Family Counseling and tell her I suggested it." She scribbled Lorraine's number on a piece of paper and handed it to me.

"Thanks, I'll call her tomorrow." I responded. Each day I put off calling until I finally got up the nerve to call five days later.

I dialed the phone and asked for Lorraine.

"Lorraine Costa," she answered.

I took a gulp and said, "Hi, my name is Pat Hastings. My teacher, Linda Corrente recommended I call you. I'd like to make an appointment to see you."

"Are you looking for counseling?" she asked.

"Oh no, I'm looking for employment. Are you hiring now?"

She hesitated at first and then said, "Can you come in for an appointment next week?"

"Just tell me the time and I'll be there," I said, surprised and happy.

When I hung up the phone, I let out a big scream. She'd actually sounded interested. There were butterflies in my stomach as I drove my car to the appointment the next week.

God, if this is your will, please open the door and if not, close it, I silently prayed.

The interview went smoothly and they seemed interested in hiring me.

"Pat, we're looking for a part-time counselor to work in the new agency we're opening up next month. We're placing an ad in tomorrow's newspaper advertising the position."

"Would you consider me for the position? It's exactly what I'm looking for."

"Definitely, you're a strong candidate. I'll give you a call next week once we make our decision."

"Thank you for your time, Lorraine. I look forward to hearing from you." We shook hands and I left the building.

I drove home in awe of God's timing and how he led me to call at the time I did. *Maybe they won't place the ad and they'll decide to hire me,* I thought to myself.

God, I really want this job. It sounds perfect because they're willing to train me on the job and I can still continue my schooling. Please open the door.

I wasn't expecting to hear Lorraine's voice when I answered the phone the next day.

"Hi Pat, this is Lorraine Costa. We decided not to place the ad because we want to offer you the job. Are you interested?"

"Am I interested?" I blurted out. "I'm thrilled. Thank you so much. When do I start?"

"We'd like you to start May first, will that work for you?"

"Yes, that will be fine."

God opened the door and I walked through. I finished college and graduated with my bachelor's degree several years later. And then I went on to get my master's degree.

I worked at the agency for six years and enjoyed every minute of it. When I tell people I treat alcoholics and drug addicts, they look at me in a funny way and say, "that must be really difficult."

"No, it's not at all. I love what I do and the patients I work with. It's a privilege to be a part of someone's life and see them change. Yes, there is relapse and struggle, but when someone understands they have a disease that can be in remission, miracles happen."

Six years later, I didn't want to look for another job, but I knew I needed to because of the changes that were taking place when we merged with another substance abuse agency. All they talked about was "time management." Paper work increased and everything we did had to be documented, even going to the rest room! I dragged my feet for awhile and wasn't looking for another job yet, hoping it would get better.

God, what do you want me to do? I know I have to do something because it's getting worse and I'm unhappy. Please lead me.

I called Barbara Varella, the director of a women's residential substance abuse agency to inquire about bed availability for one of my patients. Out-patient treatment had failed and she needed a higher level of care. Barbara and I played phone tag for over a week and finally connected to discuss the patient. We were about to hang up when she asked,

"Pat, do you know of anyone who is looking for a job? We need a new head counselor for our program."

I blurted out, "Me."

"Really. Can you come for an interview this week?"

"Sure. When?"

"How's tomorrow morning at nine?"

"I'll be there."

I went home, updated my resume and prayed. I didn't sleep well that night thinking about the interview and what I wanted to say. I drove to the appointment the next day with butterflies in my stomach because this was the first time meeting Barbara.

Just be yourself Pat. There's nothing to be nervous about. You'll do fine, I told myself.

I walked slowly up the driveway and knocked on the big red door. A young woman answered the door and smiled, "How can I help you?"

"My name is Pat Hastings. I have an appointment with the director."

"Come in. Barbara's expecting you." She led me into a small waiting room and asked me to have a seat. When Barbara entered the room, I stood up to shake her hand. She looked puzzled and then without much apparent thought she blurted out, "You're not the counselor I thought I was talking to on the phone yesterday."

"I'm not?" Neither one of us knew what to do as we stood there awkwardly for a few seconds. Then we both burst out laughing at the mishap.

"I guess you're the person I'm supposed to interview." I followed her to her office and sat down. I breathed a sigh of relief as the interview began. The butterflies were gone and I felt relaxed and calm. The interview went smoothly as I answered her questions with ease and confidence.

"Pat, I'm impressed with your resume. I have two more women that I'm interviewing this week and then I'll make my decision. I'll call you next week."

"Thank you, I really enjoyed talking with you Barbara. I think this would be a good fit for both of us and I would love to work here." We shook hands and said goodbye.

God, it seems like you're opening a door – and with a sense of humor. I know I would enjoy working there. Please open the door.

I waited with bated breath until I received the phone call a week later.

"Pat, you have a phone call from Barbara Varella on line three," the secretary announced. I hurried to my office, closed my door and took a deep breath.

"Hi Barbara," I tried to sound relaxed as my throat tightened.

"Hi Pat, this is Barbara Varella from the substance abuse treatment program. After some small talk she said, I'd like to offer you the job as head counselor. When can you start?"

"I'll give my two weeks notice today and can start on September eighth."

Thank you God for opening the door. You are faithful and I am so grateful for Your guidance and love.

Another GODincidence. God answers prayer and leads in mysterious ways. When I'm trusting God and asking to be led, things happen in the spirit world that I'm unaware of. There is a plan and all I need to do is follow it. God will open and close the door when I pray for His will and guidance.

Five years later, I encountered a similar situation with my job—another merger and all kinds of changes within the company. We were required to work over time and weren't compensated for the extra time. I even worried that I might be laid off.

It's time to move on again and I need to find another job, I told myself. *Please God show me where to look and open the door.*

The following week, I accompanied one of my patients to a doctor's appointment. While there, I ran into an old colleague I hadn't seen in several years. We chatted for awhile catching up on old news. As we said goodbye, and almost as an after thought, she asked, "Pat, have you heard about the job opening at the hospital right across the street?"

"No, I don't know anything about it. Was it in the newspaper?" I asked.

"Yes, Sunday. It sounds like a good job with great benefits. I can't apply because I don't have a masters. Do you?"

"Yes, I just earned my masters degree from Springfield College last month."

"You should apply. You'd be great with all your experience."

"Thanks. I'll check the paper when I get home." I raced home anxious to find the ad.

How could I have missed it when I read the newspaper the other day? I chided myself. I quickly thumbed through the ads and finally found it—there, it was in big bold letters "Addiction Therapist." As I read over the ad, I felt an excitement bubbling up inside of me.

The next day as I walked onto the grounds of the hospital to get an application, I felt something deep inside of me shift. I knew in my heart that I was going to get the job. I don't know how I knew it, but I did. I had a feeling of "inner knowing" and conviction that the job was mine. I filled out the application that day and sent it off.

God, I know in my heart that I'm going to get this job. I trust that it is You, and You want me to have faith.

They called me for an interview a couple weeks later. The interview went very well and they appeared to like me. "Pat, we'll call you as soon as we make our decision."

The weeks seemed to drag on as I waited patiently to hear about the job. I kept praying and trusting. Then one day, the call finally came, "Pat, this is Joan Lynch from the Human Services department at the hospital. We'd like to offer you the position as Addiction Therapist. There are a few things that need to be worked out before we give you a letter and a starting date. I'll call you next week."

Even though I didn't have a starting date and letter in hand, I threw caution to the wind. I called my present employer and gave my two weeks notice.

On the last day of work, I received a phone call from the Chief of the Substance Abuse department at the hospital. *This doesn't sound good,* I thought to myself.

"Pat, we're having some internal problems that have nothing to do with you. I'm sorry but we have to put the job on hold for another week until we work this out." She tried to be reassuring. "We really want to hire you and I'm sure it will be worked out. Please be patient."

I hung up the phone and went into a tailspin.

I can't believe this is happening God, what's going on? They offered me the job, how can they back out now? What am I going to do for money if I don't get this job after already quitting my job?

In the middle of a divorce and living alone for the first time in thirty years, I began to freak out inside and wondered if I could support myself.

God, help me to let go of control and trust You. You have a plan and You have never let me down.

After the initial panic and fearful thoughts, I calmed myself down and tried to make some sense out of it all. That feeling of knowing when I walked on the grounds to get the application was still there. I waited, prayed and surrendered. Finally, peace came and I knew God's grace was sustaining me. The next few days seemed like an eternity. Then the call finally came.

"Pat, everything worked out and the job is yours. Can you start in two weeks?"

"Yes, I'll be there Monday morning at eight. Thank you."

Flooded with gratefulness for how God worked it out, I shouted for joy and called my best friend Carole to tell her the good news. God opened the door, tested my faith and strengthened my faith in Him. God's timing and plan is perfect.

I Am a Woman Giving Birth to Myself

JOURNAL PAGE

When have I been led to the right person or place? How did it feel?

_____

_____

_____

_____

_____

_____

_____

_____

_____

_____

_____

_____

_____

_____

_____

_____

_____

_____

_____

XI

Dancing
∼ *With God* ∼

Unearth the Inner Dancer

Every year, I look forward to attending the women's spirituality retreat in Narragansett, RI overlooking the ocean. The renovated retreat house was a beautiful setting for a retreat. I loved watching the sunrise from my bedroom window as I listened to the waves crashing over the rocks.

On Friday night, the retreat leader Diane invited us to share our gifts with the other women on the retreat.

I'm not an artist. I don't write poems. God, I don't have any gifts to share. Then I heard the small still voice of God say:

YOU CAN SHARE YOUR DANCE.

But God, I only dance in my living room for You where I'm comfortable. Do you really want me to share my dance with these women?

YES, I heard quietly in my spirit.

Dancing is a part of my prayer and I love to dance. I love twirling around with God and worshiping Him in prayer and song.

Okay God, I'll tell Diane that I do spiritual dancing. I just hoped she wouldn't take me up on the offer.

The next morning at breakfast, I mentioned my dance to Diane. "You invited us to share our gifts during the weekend and I want to let you know that I dance."

"Thanks Pat. What kind of dancing do you do?" she asked.

"I do spiritual dance and I once danced in a church for a women's benefit."

Several women shared drawings and poetry during the weekend. I thought I was off the hook and breathed a sigh of relief until Diane approached me smiling early Sunday morning.

"Pat, will you share your dance with us at the closing ceremony?"

"Share my dance? I didn't think you wanted me to dance. You hadn't said anything all weekend."

"I'm sorry I didn't speak with you sooner, but will you do it? I think the women would enjoy it."

"Yes."

It came out of my mouth before I could even think about it. It must have been the spirit because inside I was shaking.

As I walked away, reality hit me and the inner dialogue began.

God, what did I get myself into? Why did I open my big mouth in the first place? I can't dance. I'm not prepared. I don't have a song to dance to and I don't have anything to wear.

I went off to my room and prayed. In my spirit I knew I wanted to dance, but I was afraid that I would look foolish.

God, please help me. I need courage to do Your will. You have given me a gift to dance and I want to be Your instrument. I want to glorify You. In my mind's eye, I pictured myself dancing for God and feeling totally at peace.

After I prayed, something inside of me shifted. A calm and peace came over me as ideas started popping into my head.

I have spiritual tapes in my car and I knew I could find one to dance to. I can borrow the long flowing skirt Diane wore yesterday. It will be perfect to dance in as I move around in my dance.

After asking Diane to borrow her skirt and getting my tapes from the car, I returned to my room to be quiet and meditate. I listened to the song and slowly began to move as dance and the spirit took over. Although I attended the presentations the rest of the day, I couldn't concentrate on what was being said. I could only think about dancing and I saw myself dancing gracefully with ease and delight.

As the women gathered in a circle for the closing ceremony, Diane invited me to come in to the middle of the circle to dance. I closed my eyes and quietly prayed, *God, I want You to be glorified,* and slowly walked into the circle.

God's grace and peace surrounded me like a warm blanket on a cold night. Being totally in the present moment, I wasn't conscious of the women watching me. My body moved gracefully as I felt the spirit of God dancing through me. The sacredness of the moment and the power of God filled my being. When I finished the dance, I bowed and thanked God for His magnificent power.

One by one, the women approached me to thank me for sharing my gift of dance.

"I'd love to dance like that. Where did you go to school?"

I answered with a smile, "My living room."

"Thank you Pat. You'll never know what you did for me. Your dance touched my heart deeply. I haven't been able to cry the whole weekend and when I watched you dance, the flood gates opened."

When Diane came over to thank me for dancing and to hug me good-bye, the words tumbled out of my mouth.

"Diane, I want to lead a spirituality retreat and show the women how to dance in the spirit. What do you think"?

"It's a great idea. You have a gift and God wants to use you as His instrument. I'll pray for you."

"Thank you," I replied. We all said good-bye to one another and left the retreat feeling renewed and refreshed.

God, thank you for giving me the courage to say yes and step out in faith. My heart is full and I want to share my dance with others. Where can I share this gift? Please open a door for this to happen.

A month later Diane called me unexpectedly. "Pat, I'm wondering if you can help me?"

"Sure. What do you need?"

"I'm scheduled to lead a women's spirituality retreat in New Hampshire next month. Something just came up and I'm unable to lead it. The retreat is for woman in 12 step recovery programs. I know you work with women in recovery and you told me that you wanted to do a retreat. Would you be able to do it for me?"

"I've never led a retreat before. I'm not sure I can do it."

"I know you can. Don't worry, I'll help you."

"Let me pray about it and I'll get back to you tomorrow."

God, I know this is what I prayed for. I want to lead a retreat and share my dance, but I'm petrified because I've never done it before. Are You opening the door?"

I knew deep in my spirit what I needed to do - step out in faith and trust that God would provide all that I needed. I called Diane the next day, "I'll do it. I think it's what God wants me to do."

The title of the retreat came to me in prayer—*I Am a Woman Giving Birth to Myself.* To my surprise, the words flowed as I prepared my presentations for twenty five women. I knew I was on the right track and being led by the hand of God. There was a special version of *Amazing Grace* that I wanted to play on the weekend. When I walked into the Christian bookstore, *Amazing Grace* was playing —and the version that I wanted.

My spiritual partner Carole accompanied me to the retreat. We delighted in the three hour drive to the retreat house in New Hampshire, admiring the leaves on the trees in their fall finery.

Several of the women greeted us at the retreat house when we arrived on Friday night. We all went out to dinner before the retreat to discuss the schedule and logistics for the weekend. Although I had some butterflies in my stomach, I felt confident that God led me there and would use me as His instrument.

As the women started to arrive, I could see apprehension and fear on their faces. They were clearly disappointed not to see Diane. They trusted her. She'd led the retreat for several years and they were accustomed to her style. They didn't know anything about me and I'm sure they wondered whether they'd get much out of the retreat.

Friday night came off without a hitch as I described our schedule and the flow of the weekend to them. I shared what happened to me on my retreat and how I danced at the closing ceremony. I invited them to share their gifts during the weekend. At the end of the evening, I danced for them. You could hear a pin drop when I finished and no one said a word. They looked surprised and taken off guard. I'm sure they wondered what they were getting themselves into with this woman from Rhode Island who dances. One of the women, Lynne came up to me and said, "Pat, I'm going to leave.

This retreat is not what I'm looking for."

"Lynne, I invite you stay and give it a chance. There's nothing to be afraid of. You don't have to do anything that you don't want to do."

I talked her out of it and she ended up staying. The stress and tension I'd seen on Lynne's face when she walked in on Friday night was completely gone when the retreat ended on Sunday afternoon. She approached me with a big smile on her face at the end of the retreat and said, "Pat, thank you for talking me out of leaving on Friday night. Sharing your dance brought me into the presence of God. I learned to play and let my hair down, which I haven't done in a long time. I didn't think I could dance, nor did I want to on Friday night. When we danced last night together and had fun, I experienced a freedom I haven't known before. I feel like a new women and my relationship with God has deepened."

I danced at the closing ceremony on Sunday afternoon as our group of twenty five women held hands in the circle and looked into each other's eyes. There was a sacred bond amongst us that hadn't been there on Friday night. Together, we thanked God for His healing power and mighty presence.

Saying "yes" to God and taking a risk to dance has opened up many doors for me. I've been leading women's spirituality retreats for the last seven years. And, yes we all dance in the Spirit.

I Am a Woman Giving Birth to Myself

JOURNAL PAGE

When have I overcome a fear to use my gifts and talents?

_____

_____

_____

_____

_____

_____

_____

_____

_____

_____

_____

_____

_____

_____

_____

_____

_____

_____

_____

XII

Finding
～ *My Voice* ～

When the Student is Ready,
the Teacher Will Appear

I continued my trips in Bermuda for many years to follow. As I said to my friend Joanne,

"I'm going on a retreat."

"Where are you going?" she asked.

"Bermuda."

She smiled and said, "Now that's the kind of retreat I'd like to go on."

Every May, I looked forward to getting away with God to just BE. I felt alive and each moment felt magical as I strolled along the beautiful pink beaches. There were no distractions, just me and God. God often spoke powerfully to me giving me direction and consolation for my life. I enjoyed the beauty around me, especially the flowering plants growing everywhere and the turquoise ocean water that took my breath away.

I always stayed at Que Sera Guest House, a lovely guest house surrounded by opulent gardens with luscious deep colored purple flowers. I swam each morning before eating my breakfast in the pool right outside my patio door. It felt like I was in paradise and I had tasted a little bit of heaven.

While in prayer one day, I heard the small still voice of God say:

I WANT YOU TO START WRITING AGAIN AND FINISH YOUR BOOK. I WILL BRING PEOPLE IN YOUR LIFE THAT WILL HELP YOU.

But God, I put my book to bed over a year ago. I'm not sure I can do it.

More than anything, I wanted to do God's will and trust Him. I knew in my heart that if God was asking me to write a book, He would give me what I needed. I prayed and asked for willingness to take the next step. A few days later, I picked up pen and paper and started to write again. My writing was sporadic, sometimes months would go by between paragraphs.

One month after my Bermuda trip, I joined Toastmasters to help me become a better speaker. I faithfully attended meetings twice a month and saw myself growing in confidence as well as skill.

One year later, I met Dayna at a Toastmaster's meeting. I introduced myself to her as we walked out at the end of the meeting.

"Hi, I'm Pat. Is this your first meeting?"

"Yes, it is. My name in Dayna."

"How did you like the meeting?" I asked.

"I liked it a lot. You look familiar," she commented.

"You too."

"I think I know your son. Is his name Tim?"

"Yes, how do you know Tim?" I asked.

"I had a blind date with him in the summer."

"How did you know I was his mother?" I asked curiously.

"I guessed. When you gave your speech tonight you talked about one of your sons moving to Boise, Idaho. Tim told me on our date that he wanted to move to Boise. I put two and two together. Did he move yet?"

"Yes. He moved last month and loves it there."

We continued our conversation in the parking lot. "Dayna, I'm leading a women's spirituality retreat next month – I'd love for you to join us. Here's the brochure."

"Thanks, I'll look it over," she answered. "Here's my brochure for a rebirthing workshop I'm leading next Sunday."

I glanced over her brochure without really understanding what rebirthing was, but signed up on the spot because it fell on Mother's Day. I suspected it would help me connect with my own mother who died thirty nine years ago.

That night, I wrote in my journal. "Pat, pay attention to synchronicity." I sensed deep within that God was leading me. I had no way of knowing that this path was the beginning of deep inner healing and transformation.

During my first rebirthing session, my whole body vibrated with energy. I felt God's divine energy flowing through me like I'd never experienced before. I intended to connect with my mother spiritually and that's what happened.

While I breathed, in my mind's eye, I saw my mother with God, happy and free. I floated in the air as angels and loved ones surrounded me. I didn't want to leave that sacred place because of the joy and ecstasy I felt. I didn't know much about this rebirthing, but I loved it and wanted more.

As I looked back over Dayna's brochure, I had a better understanding of what it was all about. It stated that 70% of the body's toxins are released through the breath, flooding the body with oxygen that purifies both physical and emotional bodies. While this simple process released stored emotions from the body, it also stimulated memory function in the brain.

By learning to breathe consciously, one is able to uncover and release forgotten or subconscious thought patterns that create limitations in life. Rebirthing cleanses your mind and body in a very dynamic way with Divine Energy.

Sondra Ray in her book *Pure Joy* states that "Rebirthing acquaints you with a dimension of spiritual energy which you have never experienced. It can be the ultimate healing experience because breath, together with quality of thoughts, can produce miracles. Rebirthing increases your ability to receive love and can definitely improve relationships. Rebirthing is truly a rejuvenation process. Your body is rejuvenated with divine energy. Rebirthing is a sacred experience." (Ray, Celestial Arts, 1988)

Every month I attended the group rebirthing sessions because I liked how I felt afterwards. I felt a shift in my thinking and with that came more joy and peace in my life. After six months of group sessions, I decided to try individual rebirthing sessions with Dayna. I didn't know there were emotional blocks and false beliefs that were blocking me from moving forward and creating my heart's desires and dreams, but God did.

It became clear to me after the first rebirthing session with Dayna that fear blocked me from moving forward and completing my book. As I began to recognize and release the self-defeating thoughts, my fear dissipated. Rebirthing dispelled my beliefs and thoughts of not being good enough and smart enough. Growing up in my home with two alcoholic parents, I learned that what I had to say wasn't important. I shut up and said nothing. I didn't feel safe to talk about the fighting and yelling when my parents drank. Through the rebirthing, I found my voice and began using it. I had tapped into a new energy that was very empowering.

I replaced self-defeating thoughts with affirmations that Dayna helped me create.

I now release all patterns of fear and withholding to you the Holy Spirit for healing.

I repeat the affirmations to myself, as well as write them down in my journal. Each rebirthing session brought about powerful changes in me.

I felt propelled to move forward with increased energy and passion. My writing exploded and my creativity flowed. I couldn't wait to sit and write. I'd wake up in the middle of the night with paper and pen next to my bed and write things down. It felt like the words came from a deep well within, a previously untapped source of creativity.

After six months of rebirthing, I found myself on an accelerated fast track of inner healing, transformation and empowerment. I wrote more in six months than I did in six years. With my energy unblocked, I move forward with confidence and boldness in the direction of my dreams. Not only have I made progress with my book, my relationships have improved. I'm more open and willing to receive love.

The chance meeting or GODincidence with Dayna at Toastmaster's was God's perfect timing and plan. It was a Divine connection and I know God brought Dayna there for me because it was the only Toastmaster meeting Dayna attended.

I Am a Woman Giving Birth to Myself

JOURNAL PAGE

Do I pay attention to divine guidance? Where have I been
transformed and healed? Have I found my voice yet?

_____

_____

_____

_____

_____

_____

_____

_____

_____

_____

_____

_____

_____

_____

_____

_____

_____

_____

_____

_____

XIII

You Have Everything
You Need, Just Believe

Writing the Book with God's Support

I am only a pencil in God's hand, however imperfect I am,
God writes through me beautifully   (Mother Theresa)

"You should write a book about your faith and how God provides; you are the most faithful woman I know. God just seems to answer your prayers. Have you always been like this?" my friend Michele commented. As I pondered the question for a minute, I answered, "Yes, I guess I have been."

God's been *hounding* me for over twenty five years to write a book. I knew deep down in my heart that someday I would write a book. God's been loving and patient with me. He's waited for me to say "yes" and trust that I had all I needed to write a book and do His will. Facing my fears and believing in myself has been a journey of self discovery and deepened faith. God's provided each step of the way as I've been able to let go and trust the process. I have a quote on my desk that speaks to my heart.

"You must do the thing you think you cannot do."
(Eleanor Roosevelt)

Finally, in June 1990, I told my coworker, Susan, "I'm writing a book."

"I didn't know you could write."

"Neither did I," I answered. I didn't think I could write a book, but I knew that if God was calling me to do it, He would guide me and bring me the people I needed to help me with it.

How many times will I start and stop writing? Until I finish. I promise God. I say yes to You. I will be obedient.

When I started writing my story seven years ago, I randomly opened my bible to a scripture passage. I often reflect upon the words when I'm struggling with inadequacy.

At the beginning, I foretell the outcome. In advance things not yet done. My plan shall stand, I accomplish my every purpose. Yes, I have spoken, I will accomplish it and I will do it. (Isaiah 46:10)

God has a plan and all I have to do is follow it. I had to remember that writing a book was God's plan, not mine. Sounds easy, right? Not so, when you have no idea what you're doing. I'd write for months and then put my writing down for a year at a time because I became discouraged. This pattern went on for six years until I got serious about my writing, changed my thinking, and took steps to make it happen.

You're wasting your time. No one would read it. You're not a writer. What do you have to say that anyone would want to read?

Fear ruled my life. Fear that I wouldn't do it perfectly and it wouldn't be *good enough*. The old tapes of inadequacy, of not being good enough played in my head day after day.

I began my writing after reading and completing the exercises in Julia Cameron's book, *The Artists Way*. The author writes "when we open ourselves to our creativity, we open ourselves to the creator's creativity within us and our lives. Creativity is God's gift to us. Using our creativity is our gift back to God. When we open ourselves to exploring our creativity, we open ourselves to God: good orderly direction. Our creative dreams and yearnings come from a divine source. As we move toward our dreams, we move toward our divinity." (Cameron, 1992 Penquin)

I learned a lot about myself through completing the exercises recommended by the author. My negative self talk blocked me from my creativity. I needed to change the messages I gave to myself if I was going to succeed.

Rather than trusting my intuition, my talent, my skills, my desires, I had feared where my Creator might take me with my creativity and I gave up. "We all have an inner artist, but many of us weren't encouraged to explore it growing up." (Cameron, 1992) I had no idea of what I was capable of doing or creating.

In the process of completing the exercises, I learned the importance of surrendering my need to control the result and changed my thinking from self-doubt to self expression. Cameron writes "God knows that the sky's the limit. Anyone honest will tell you that possibility is far more frightening than impossibility, that freedom is far more terrifying than any prison." (Cameron 1992)

A few months after completing the course, I received a monthly catalog in the mail and noticed an online course that I'd never seen before, *Writing Your Life Story*. The course was for beginner writers who wanted to start writing their story. I took the next step and signed up. Fear struck and I wanted to quit after reading the first assignment. I made a commitment to myself to keep going and ride out the fear.

I faithfully completed the exercises until the third class when I started to question my abilities.

Am I on the right track, God?

We were encouraged to write in questions or comments on the material presented. I took a risk and asked the teacher, "Do you think I'm on the right track?"

"Definitely. You're further along than you could ever imagine. Doubts are normal. Trust your instincts-you have an important story to tell and you can do it. You're in a safe place to spread your wings."

With her encouragement, my writing became more frequent and I began to enjoy writing. Although encouragement is an important part of the process, I had to stop looking outside of myself for others to say I was *good enough*. I had to stop comparing myself to others and start believing in myself. I wanted to trust that I was doing God's will and that He would give me all that I needed to write a book *one step at a time*. I needed to let the process happen and go with the flow.

God speaks to me through the book

I found the book *One Day My Soul Just Opened Up* by Iyanla Vanzant at a yard sale six months earlier. I decided to take it to my daily prayer and read a chapter at a time. The morning after I realized I was comparing myself to my classmates, the chapter I read was *Being Authentic.* The author wrote "Authenticity demands no comparisons. You cannot compare yourself or what you do to anyone else. You are you! You represent a true and original part of the Master. There is no one else like you. To the degree that you compare yourself to others and govern your actions by the actions of others, you will be lost. Authenticity means that you must do what you do the way you do it and allow everyone else the same courtesy." (Vanzant 1998 Simon & Schuster)

Not only did the author write about comparing herself to others, but she wrote about her experiences with becoming a writer. She wanted to be a famous writer and copied others styles, which almost drove her crazy. She finally came to a place where she writes the way she writes, dresses the way she dresses.

Although I enjoyed the class and learned a lot, I decided to take a break from my writing when I finished the online class. Preparing for a women's spirituality retreat took most of my time. I felt relieved that I didn't have to write. *I'm just taking a break,* I told myself. *When the retreat is over, I'll get back to my writing.* I wasn't looking forward to it though. I planned on giving myself two weeks of rest after the retreat before I started writing again.

Stuck again. I developed all kinds of excuses why I didn't have the time to write. The house had to be cleaned, even though I hated cleaning. When I did force myself to sit and write, it took hours just to get a paragraph down. I prayed to get back on track and finish what I started.

God speaks to me through a Christmas present

I couldn't wait to open my friend Sandra's Christmas present because it was wrapped so beautifully. I loved the two angels on the *Angelic Embrace* cover of the instrumental CD. I played the CD the next morning in prayer. I expected to hear quiet soothing music to meditate with. Instead, in the middle of the instrumentals, I heard a song playing. I listened carefully to the words as my spirit sensed there was a message for me.

"Release me from my shroud, to put myself in a higher state. See the love, the truth. Look inside, see the vision from above. Release me to see the meaning of it all." (Angelic Embrace, Halo 1995)

I didn't understand what the message meant for my life at first. Shortly afterwards, while in prayer on New Year's Day, I randomly picked an angel card from the Angelic Messenger Cards. (Young-Sowers 1993)

Angel of Release

"The card is calling you to recognize that you may be sinking or "stuck" in the quicksand of your rational dialogue and it is your cue to move into the perspective of your divine nature. You have drawn this card to help you validate your inner feelings about the "work" you are already doing, want to do or dream about creating that is your gift to humanity. This is a critical card of alignment because it calls you to accept your own guidance and a spiritual perspective to your life. Consider this card as an affirmation of your immediate ability to claim your highest self and release the needy aspects of your life that mentally hold you prisoner." (Young- Sowers1993)

Please God show me the needy aspects of myself that keep me imprisoned and need healing. It became clear that I didn't trust myself and I wanted others to tell me what to do. I didn't trust the God and wisdom within.

I still doubted my ability to write a book. God told me through the song to rise above my limitations, to accept my divine nature. I prayed and meditated on the message.

God speaks to me through songs

The words of a song caught my ear while exercising at Curves gym a few days later. I'd never heard it before and the words kept repeating themselves over and over again.

"You are annointed and I have a plan. You are annointed and

I have a plan." (World Wide Message Tribe, The year of the Lord's favour lyrics)

Although there were other words in the song, those were the only words I heard.

Okay God, I'm getting the message. You're calling me to write this book. I'd better pay attention.

Just a few hours later, while driving in the car and listening to the oldies station, the words of Josh Groban's song *Believe* spoke to my heart.

"You have everything you need, just believe
You have everything you need, just believe."

God is everywhere and will use whatever it takes to get my attention. I need to do my part and leave the outcome to Him. I reminded myself that this is His plan, not mine. After hearing the two songs that spoke to my heart, I became willing and started to write again.

God wants to communicate with us and it's His desire to give us everything we need for the journey. The problem is we often don't pay attention. I'm learning to pay attention and do the next right thing without always having to figure things out first.

My daughter and I went shopping at the local thrift shop. While browsing in the used book section, a book just about jumped off the shelf at me. *Writing From Personal Experience - How To Turn Your Life Into Salable Prose* by Nancy Davidoff Kelton. What a bargain for a buck. The author shared about the importance of writing from the heart, which is what I was trying to do.

The next day my friend Gayle and I went to lunch for her birthday. While at lunch I shared, "I found a book yesterday that confirmed what I'm writing about."

"Tell me about it."

"It's about being authentic and writing from the heart."

"I'd like to write a book someday as a legacy for my children," she answered.

She thanked me for the journal I gave her for her birthday. "I think it's a message that it's time to start writing."

We spotted the angel cards on the counter while browsing

around the gift shop after lunch. I randomly picked a card—Archangel Gabriel "Writer's Inspiration." The message was about the importance of writing in a journal. I knew that message was for both of us.

Later that week, I received an email from the author Arielle Ford introducing her new CD and resource guide—"Successful Secrets To Becoming An Author—Everything you should know about publishing, publicity and building a platform." The CDs and one hundred and eighty page resource guide promised an inside blueprint to jump start your career as author and speaker. It seemed like the next step to move forward until I saw the price $499.00 (it was 100% guaranteed and could be sent back if it wasn't what you wanted.)

I signed up for the course and received the CDs and booklet. You would think with the messages and affirmations I received from God through the Angel cards, I would be on my way and nothing would stop me. Unfortunately, just the opposite happened. I felt overwhelmed after I listened to the first CD and heard what I needed to do to publish a book. I had to go on book tours around the country, write a lengthy book proposal and have a solid marketing plan. I immediately got my money back for the course and stopped writing.

God, I don't have the desire, time or money to go forward with publishing this book. I'm not a public speaker and don't know anything about promoting my book. I work full time and don't have extra time or money. I can't travel around the country to promote the book. I'm sorry God, but I just can't do it.

I felt relieved, but discouraged about the time and money I wasted over the years on trying to write my book. I told my friends when they asked about my book, "I put my book to bed." End of story. No more pressure and it felt like a weight had been lifted.

I did follow through on one suggestion from the course. I joined Toastmasters, an international public speaking group. I wanted to improve my speaking for the women's retreats I led. I loved Toastmasters right from the start. I gained confidence in myself and saw improvement with each speech I gave. I faithfully attended meetings for a year and prepared speeches.

While I focused on speaking, I didn't think about my book at all. I never once looked at what I had written or thought about it unless someone asked me how my book was coming along. God patiently respected my timing. He allowed me to put my writing aside for awhile...But He didn't give up. That's why He's often called the "hound of heaven."

I Am a Woman Giving Birth to Myself

JOURNAL PAGE

What is the desire of my heart and vision for my life?

XIV

Passion and Fire
Move Me Forward

How to Be Successful and
Make Your Dream a Reality

Fan the flame, rekindle the embers. Stir up the gift that is
within me. (2 Timothy 1-6)

One year after I'd put my book to bed, while writing the talks for
the retreat, *Love Is Letting Go Of Fear,* God showed me clearly that I
was stuck in fear and that's why I put the book to bed. YUK. I didn't
like admitting this to myself and especially to the women coming on
the retreat. I sat with the fear and trusted God to lead.

Okay God, show me the way. What do I need to do next?

When I'm open and ask for help, God shows me the way. He
opens the door. A week later, I attended a Toastmasters meeting
and volunteered for table topics where a person is asked to speak
on an unknown subject for one to two minutes. Two minutes can be
a long time when you have no idea what to say. My question was:

"What are you afraid of and what are you going to do about it?"

The words flowed effortlessly. "I'm afraid of finishing and publishing my book. I put my book to bed a year ago because of fear. I
don't know what I'm going to do about it, but I'm willing to be led."
I faced my fear and trusted that God would lead me.

Two days later, I attended my first International Toastmasters
Conference. I signed up for the setting goals workshop because
the presenter was a published author. I got goose bumps and the
hairs on my arms stood up when she began talking about the steps
she took to self-publish her first book. I couldn't contain myself

and wanted to jump up as the tears flowed down my cheeks. Up until then, I knew nothing about self-publishing. Another GODincidence—I knew what I needed to do next.

During her presentation, the speaker showed us her Picture Book with her dreams and intentions in it. Some people call it a treasure map or a dream board. Her book had pictures of her at book signings and speaking to audiences. Her intentions, dreams and favorite quotes were in her book.

I couldn't wait to get home and start my Picture Book. Deep within, I knew creating my Picture Book would move me forward. It would help me tap into the energy and power I needed to succeed. I left the conference with a new vision and enthusiasm to do what God was asking me to do—move forward, finish and publish my book.

I create my reality by my thoughts, feelings and positive attitudes. I needed to see my book published in my mind's eye before it happened. I had to conceive it on the inside first before it would happen on the outside. When I meditated, I felt joy and exhilaration as I imagined holding my book in my hands for the first time. I didn't succeed up until then because I didn't see myself as a writer. I told myself people wouldn't read my book and I was wasting my time. I needed to develop spiritual vision—seeing through the eyes of faith.

The day after the conference I worked on my Picture Book for hours. I cut out pictures and words from magazines. I wrote out favorite quotes and scriptures. I read my Picture Book faithfully every day in prayer, sometimes more than once a day when I started to doubt myself and the process. My intention is on the front page.

My intention is to complete and publish my book "Simply a Woman of Faith" by 6-07.

(I sent my book to the publisher June 1—right on schedule.)

I contacted a publishing company and learned all about self-publishing and publishing on demand. You don't have to put out thousands of dollars and lose it if your book doesn't sell. They print the books when they are needed, not before. I liked what they had to offer. They had several plans to choose from when I was ready to publish my book. I called the company and they sent me a sample book. I wasn't impressed with the quality of the work. There were many other self-publishing companies that I planned to research.

After the conference, something had shifted inside of me in such a short time. I felt a renewed energy to start writing *again*. I faced my fear, changed my thinking and asked for help. I trusted God would open the doors as I moved in faith and trusted the process.

With enthusiasm and confidence, I told my friends and family, "I'm getting my book published." Although I felt determined, I knew there was still a lot I didn't know. My faith was tested often during the process of writing. Faith is knowing I'm being guided and given everything I need to accomplish the task. I often felt overwhelmed that I didn't have enough faith. During one of those moments, I poured out my heart to God and wrote my feelings and thoughts in my journal.

God, I'm feeling overwhelmed and alone. Why did you choose me to write a book? I'm not a business woman. I know nothing about publishing and marketing. I'm in over my head. I want someone to hold my hand and tell me what to do. I'm afraid of making the wrong decisions. Do I self-publish or look for a traditional publisher? I think you want me to self-publish, but each company has something differ-ent to offer. I'm confused. All the books I've read say I should have a marketing plan before I even start to write the book. I don't have a clue how I'm going to market this book. I need help.

I went to work that day with a heavy heart, trying to shake off the negativity and overwhelming feelings I experienced. I opened the conference room first thing in the morning and noticed *People* magazine lying on the table. I picked it up to throw it away. Instead of throwing it away, I opened a page and my eyes fell to:

I have a plan to make all of your dreams come true

I sat down, put my head on the table and cried like a baby. I needed God's heavenly touch to get me back on track. I cut the words out of the magazine and they remain on my desk as a remind-er that this is God's plan, not mine.

My life is unfolding according to a Divine Plan

God showed me I was trying too hard to make it happen. There are times when resting is the answer, not forcing things to happen. When I didn't have all the answers of *how* it was going to happen, I became frightened and overwhelmed. God showed me I didn't have to know *how* to do it, the *how* would show up when it was the right time. It didn't have to be so hard when I allowed God to lead me to the next step and the right people. I wanted to control God, rather than allowing Him to lead me and bring the answers to me. I needed to learn to keep my thoughts on my desires and dreams and away from my fears.

When I pray, meditate and visualize, my answers come. Maybe not in that moment, but the answers do come. It may be a thought or an impulse to follow up on something or call someone. When I visualize my intentions in prayer, God then gives me the impulse to act on them. Like the time I called Rushnell Squire, the author of *When God Winks.*

I visualized myself speaking with Rushnell on the phone, asking him for an endorsement for my book.

My heart pounded as I waited for someone to pick up the phone. One, two, three rings, then the answering machine picks up. The message is interrupted by a voice in the middle of the message.

"Hello, wait a minute until I get this machine turned off."

"I'd like to speak with Rushnell, is this he?"

"This is Rushnell, who's this?"

I blurted out, "Oh my God, a real voice, I didn't think it would be this easy. My name is Pat Hastings and I just finished writing my manuscript, *Simply a Woman of Faith.* Would you be willing to read it and provide an endorsement?"

"Sure. Send me your manuscript and I'll read it."

The conversation flowed like we were old buddies. He told me how God worked in his life with his book, *When God Winks.*

"How did you get your book out there and market it?" I asked.

"I knew someone who knew someone who helped me get on the TV show *Hour of Power.* That was my break and the book sold in all the bookstores after that. My wife and I stepped out in faith and put out quite a bit of money to make it happen."

I got off the phone and took a gulp of air. I thanked God for His guidance and opening the door. I mailed the manuscript the next day.

God, I don't know anyone to ask for help like Rushnell did. I heard the small still voice of God say:

YOU KNOW ME.

"Oh yeah, I forgot about you" and burst out laughing.

Due to his busy schedule and prior publishing commitments, I didn't receive his endorsement before my book went to press.

Writing my book has taught me a lot about myself. I say *I can't* do something and then when I try, I do okay, sometimes more than okay. I'm learning to change those two little words from *I can't* to *I can* and then - wait for the miracle.

I kept saying to myself and whoever would listen,"writing this book is so hard. It's the hardest thing I've ever done." Then I learned about the law of attraction. If I believed it was hard and kept saying it to myself, it would continue to be hard. What I say comes back to me. I produced an unconscious negative intention. What you think about, you bring about. Instead of saying how hard writing was, I changed my intention.

My intention is to be peaceful and have fun writing by book. My intention is to be God's instrument and share His love with the world.

Along with changing my thinking, I created a Picture Board for my dining room wall. My son Jimmy visited one day and said, "Mom, what's Oprah doing on your dining room wall?"

I smiled and said, "I'm going to be on the Oprah show with my book."

He shrugged his shoulders and said "Oh, that's nice."

My friend and I chatted about writing my book while exercising at Curves gym one day. She asked, "Have you heard about the Book Coach, Lisa Tener?"

"Never," I answered.

"I'll call you later with her number."

"Thanks, I'll check her out."

Two days later, I received a phone call from a friend whom I hadn't spoken to in several years. "I'm writing a book," I told her, my excitement hard to contain.

"Do you know of the Book Coach, Lisa Tener?"

PAY ATTENTION, PAT. I'M SPEAKING TO YOU.

I called Lisa immediately. She told me about a new teleconference class starting in two weeks on how to write your book in 60 days. The price of the class was five hundred and eighty eight dollars. We weren't sure if this was the right class for me since most of my book was already written. Lisa assured me that I could get my money back if this didn't fit my needs or we could switch to private coaching, which is what I eventually ended up doing.

God, where am I going to get the money for the class?

I purchased some stocks several years ago and decided to sell them a few months earlier. I received a check for two thousand two hundred dollars from the credit union which enabled me to catch up on all my bills. The money was spent in no time. A month after I sold the stocks and received my money, I received another statement stating I had two thousand three hundred dollars in my account. *There must be a mistake, I'll call tomorrow and find out.*

"This is Pat Hastings and I'd like you to please check the balance in my account."

"Sure. Please wait while I check."

"Thanks." I answered.

"Mrs. Hastings, you have a balance of two thousand three hundred dollars."

"Are you sure?"

"Yes, is there a problem?"

"No. No problem at all."

I don't know how that happened, but it did. God works mysteriously. The money was there all the time, but I never saw it and didn't know it was in there. For whatever reason, it wasn't on the monthly statement that I received each month (or I just didn't see it because I probably would have spent it.)

The money came after I signed up for the teleconference class. I stepped out in faith, trusting God would provide. He provided the money for the class and the thousand dollars to pay for the publishing when I was ready. The doors were opening wide for me to keep going and writing.

I wrote diligently for several months. I love it when the juices are flowing and I wake up in the middle of the night with an idea or a way to say something better. I quickly jot it down on the paper next to my bed. I made a commitment to myself and Lisa that I would write a certain amount of hours each week and I stuck to it.

Eight months after the Toastmasters conference and using my Picture Book daily, I finished writing my manuscript New Years Eve. I experienced both excitement and fear at the same time. I was on top of the world and grateful to God for giving me the grace to face my fear and heal. The time had finally come for "my baby" to be born, to be brought into the world. *Am I ready, God?* Like giving birth, once labor starts, it cannot be stopped.

While in prayer New Years Eve Day I picked two angel cards from the Angelic Messenger cards. (Young-Sowers 1993)

Angel of Birth and Angel of Trust

I spent time in prayer New Years Day focusing on what I had accomplished over the past year and my intentions for the coming year. I asked God to speak to me about the future of my book and randomly picked another angel card.

Angel of Joy

"You have drawn this card because you are being guided to continue to believe in yourself and to seek success as it is emerging in your life, often in unexpected and unforeseen ways and events. Believe in your dreams because you are entering a powerful and extremely positive period in your life. You will see some of your deepest desires come to fruition. No longer afraid of failure or the judgments of others, you are ready to spread your wings and discover qualities, abilities and strengths that have been trying to emerge. Joy is an internal state of being, one that emerges from a profound belief in the sacredness of life. If you are moving into joy, it is because you have accepted that you can take a risk." (Young-Sowers 1993)

Deep in my spirit, I heard the small still voice of God say:

I WILL OPEN DOORS FOR YOU AND BRING PEOPLE TO HELP YOU WITH THE NEXT STEP OF PUBLISHING AND PROMOTING YOUR BOOK. TRUST ME.

With the manuscript complete, I needed to find an editor. Prices ranged from sixty dollars an hour to one hundred and twenty five dollars an hour. I had no idea how long it would take to edit my book and how much it would cost. I sensed it would take awhile since I had no formal training in writing. I prayed and asked God to lead me to the right editor.

"Mom, you have to change your yard sale mentality when it comes to looking for an editor."

"You're right Tim, I always want a bargain, but I'm not willing to do that with my book. I want the best editor I can find and I don't care how much it costs."

After checking out a few different editors, I called the Book Coach, Lisa Tener again. I felt a connection with her and knew in my heart that I wanted her to edit my book. She also happened to be the most expensive, but she was the best.

Okay God, where's the money going to come from? This could be very expensive by the time she's through editing.

I asked for a dream that night. In my dream I was walking up a ladder into the sky. In my spirit, I knew God was saying—*The sky's the limit.* I called Lisa the next day and hired her, trusting the money would come. A half hour later, I checked on line for the balance in my checking account. I received my paycheck the day before, but hadn't looked at it since it goes directly into the bank.

What's this extra money God? Where did it come from?

When I reached work, I asked about my last paycheck and discovered that I'd received a performance award. In the past, we'd always been informed of our awards at the awards ceremony. When the editing was complete, it turned out that the extra money covered the bill and it was exactly what I needed. My God is full of surprises and loves to shower His blessings on me when I trust Him and step out in faith.

Lisa and I started working together immediately. She guided me, encouraged me and showed me what I needed to do to make my manuscript the best it could be. Rather than just edit, she unleashed the writer in me by teaching me how good writers think, how they write and polish their work.

God led me, through Lisa's suggestion, to a graphic designer who designed the cover of my book, which I love.

My friend Joanne received an email about self publishing and forwarded the email to me. I contacted the company and liked what they had to offer. They sent me a sheet comparing their services to those of several larger self publishing companies. I had been searching for this information, but couldn't find it earlier.

The process of writing this book provided a journey of discovering parts of myself that I never knew existed – the eloquent writer, the confident writer, the thorough researcher. Rather than looking to an expert to make my decisions for me, God helped me to grow as a writer, a publisher, a speaker, a decision maker and a creative, expressive human being. It took seven years to believe in myself and for my book to be published.

God, I'm going to stay on fire, I'm going to be aglow. I'm going to be passionate about SEEING my dreams come to pass.

My passion moves me forward with ease and delight.

I Am a Woman Giving Birth to Myself

JOURNAL PAGE

What small step am I willing to take to succeed
and make my dream a reality?

XV

I Want All of You and I Will Be Enough

How to Prepare for Your Soul Mate, The God Way

God always answers prayers. He answers with a "Yes," "No" or "WAIT." I like it when my prayers are answered quickly and don't like it when I have to wait. While I'm waiting and trusting God for something, I don't usually see the wisdom in it. It becomes clear when the prayer is finally answered.

The desire of my heart is to meet my soul mate, to love and be loved. God has placed that desire in my heart and it will be fulfilled, in His time, not mine. Everyone longs to give themselves completely to someone, to have a deep soul relationship with another, to be loved thoroughly and exclusively. My spirit soars when I think about that possibility.

I received a scripture passage in 2003 after praying about my soul mate coming into my life. It's a promise from God.

For the vision still has it's time, presses onto fulfillment and will not disappoint. If it delays, wait for it, it will surely come. It will not be late. (Habakuk 2:3)

I'm grateful to God that He didn't answer my prayer in 2003. I thought I was ready, but I wasn't. Being alone and finding out who Pat is and what she wants has empowered me to become the woman God created me to be. For most of my life, I knew what everybody else wanted, but now I know what I want. I looked to others for my answers, rather than going within for my own wisdom and guidance. I've learned to trust myself and become my own best friend. I'm comfortable spending time alone and going places by myself now. I regularly take myself out to lunch and dinner and buy myself flowers when I feel the urge.

"Mom, who are you going rollerblading with today?" my son Tim asked. I surprised myself when I answered, "I'm going with my best friend, ME."

I've experienced deep inner healing and personal growth in the process of waiting, as well as a deeper relationship with God and a stronger faith. I depend on God for everything and know that He is the source for all of my needs.

God is enough and He is my all

Waiting for my soul mate hasn't been easy. I want what I want when I want it. I've complained, bargained, pleaded, cried, tried to control the process and tried to *help* God along. Like God needs my help. Letting go of fear and control has been a healing process.

God what's wrong with me? Why haven't I met my soul mate yet?

Shortly after I asked that question to God, I received an email from a friend. This is part of what it said.

"But God said: not until you are satisfied, fulfilled and content with being loved by me alone. I love you my child and until you discover that only in me is your satisfaction to be found, you will not be capable of the perfect relationship that I have planned for you. You will never be united with another until you are united with me, exclusive of any other longings or desires. I want you to stop wishing, planning and allow me to give you the most thrilling plan existing, one that you can not imagine. I want you to have the best. Please allow me to bring it to you. You just keep watching, learning and listening to the things I tell you. You must wait. Do not be anxious or worried. You must keep looking off and away, up to me, or you will miss what I want to show you. And then you will be ready. I will surprise you with a love that is far more wonderful than you could every dream of.

(This text was emailed to me and I have been unable to locate its source or determine any copywrite for the material. Any copywrite brought to the author's attention and proven, will be corrected in the next printing of the book and given correct attribution. Please forgive any error of omission.)

In my spirit, I heard the small still voice of God say:

I WANT ALL OF YOU AND I WILL BE ENOUGH.

God, will you be enough for me? I felt ready to meet my soul mate and didn't want to wait. I thought being in a relationship with a man would make me happy and complete.

Surrendering and trusting God to do what He said He will do has been a long road with lots of detours. I believed that I had to make things happen. Surrendering and trusting means giving up attachment to results. When we have an attachment to results, we have a hard time giving up control and waiting.

Why do I think I need to help God find my soul mate?

Because I'm afraid if I don't do it, it may not happen. God wants me to be peaceful and content right where I'm at and with what I have. He knows what I need and will provide when the timing is right.

Dating services work for lots of people, but that wasn't God's plan for me. I tried to help God along because He wasn't working fast enough.

I joined an expensive dating service that turned out to be a bomb. I received an ad in the mail about the dating service and it sounded interesting. I had no intention of joining, but walked out a life time member.

I found myself being drawn in as I sat across from the pleasant saleswoman who explained the dating service. She showed me pictures of couples who met and got married.

"Pat, you will have no trouble meeting guys; you are beautiful. You could be a model. I know of a few men right now who you will connect with."

"Thank you." Flattery will get you everywhere.

I thought I would meet quality men with the money that I spent. It's not like me to spend money impulsively. What was I thinking of? I met a few men through the dating service, but nothing worked out. One man told me he loved me after one week. I ran as fast as I could. Another man was divorced from his wife, but for her birthday took her to a fancy restaurant and bought her expensive jewelry.

I joined a computer dating service. For a short time, I searched it daily, and became frustrated when some men didn't answer me when I wrote to them and often the ones who chose me, I had nothing in common with. Some down right lied about things, their age, job and marital status. A few funny things happened. My date made a great impression at breakfast when he knocked the water glass over – on me. The look of horror on his face said it all. We both burst out laughing as the waitress ran around cleaning up the mess and I dried myself off.

A few scary things happened too. I communicated online with a man who seemed nice. I liked what he wrote about himself and what was important to him. Thankfully, I found out important information about him before we met. He was recently in the hospital for a mental breakdown and had a list of mental health diagnoses a mile long. Needless to say, we never met. That ended my relashionship with the dating service. I finally surrendered trying to find my soul mate and said to God:

Okay God, you do it

God wants to guide me and spare me the unnecessary pain that I often bring on myself by my impatience and fear. Fast forward one year later and I'm getting tired of waiting and being patient. I danced several nights a week and focused my radar screen on "meeting a man."

There must be something I can do to make it happen God. Maybe I heard you wrong and you don't want me to wait. After all, it's been five years.

When I'm getting off track, God gets my attention by sending me dreams. I dreamt several times about rushing and throwing things together in my suitcase. I was afraid I'd miss my plane. Packing a suitcase in my dreams means trying to get it all together.

As I worked with the dreams and prayed about it, especially the panic and rushing that I'd miss my plane, it became clear I was trying to control again. I felt afraid that if I didn't do it, my soul mate wouldn't *just show up* as God had promised. God showed me my reservations and lack of trust in His promise.

Shortly after receiving the dream, I attended a weekend retreat. There were several workshops to choose from. I chose "How to have your heart's desires manifested." When the presentation ended, the presenter led us in a guided meditation. After the meditation, we were given paper and pencil and instructed to write whatever came into our minds. I wrote a letter from God to myself:

Dear Patricia,

Be at peace, be at peace, trust, trust. Beyond your wildest dreams will your soul mate come into your life. He will come to you. You don't have to do anything, but just BE. Learn to love yourself compassionately. You are beautiful, cherished and loved. All is well and on time. Practice being in the moment. Let Joy exude from you. It is your Joy that will draw your mate. I give you the gift of Joy this day.

Love God

I allowed the words to permeate and seep into my being. I wanted peace and I wanted God's will in my life. I asked myself, what is Joy? Sometimes Joy and Peace feel the same to me. For me, Joy is a deep inner knowing that I'm exactly where I need to be and all of my needs are provided for. Joy comes naturally from within when I'm in balance and connected to God. Joy is the ability to trust God's perfect plan for my life. Joy is a sense of well being and happiness. During the day, I often pray this affirmation.

I open my heart to more Joy and Pleasure in my life

During the weekend I wrote an affirmation about manifesting my heart's desire.

"I am creating and expecting a loving, kind, joyful, spiritual, honest, healthy relationship with my soul mate. He will be playful, fun and will love to laugh. He will be as crazy about me as I am about him. We will both be growing spiritually, on the same path, sharing, growing, loving.

He will love to dance as I do and we will dance into the sunset together.

There will be no blocks or fears. We will get along fabulously. We will love each other, love being together as well as being alone."

Several months later, while attending a professional conference, I spotted a man whom I was attracted to.

"Susan, do you know that man?" I asked my friend.

"Yes, I know him. His name is Mark. He's a super guy and he's single," my friend answered. The next day at breakfast, the last day of the conference, I looked up and saw Susan pointing me out to him. I'm sure my face turned crimson red and I wanted to crawl under the table.

As I walked to the next session, I ran right into him and we both smiled and said hello. A few hours later, while waiting in line to get my food for lunch, I spotted him out of the corner of my eye standing right behind me. I almost panicked and didn't know what to do. I knew he knew of my interest in him. I took a big gulp and turned around and said,

"Hi, I'm Pat Hastings."

"I'm Mark Dougherty."

We chatted briefly until we got to the end of the line.

"I'd like to sit with you, but I'm meeting a colleague for lunch. Maybe we could talk later."

"I'd like that," I answered with a smile. We parted ways and each found our own table.

The conference was almost over and I didn't think I would run into him again because there were over four hundred people attending the conference. I felt disappointed because we hadn't made plans to meet. I took a walk after lunch and prayed *To Let Go and Let God.* As I walked to my last class, we ran into each other again on the path.

We talked for a few minutes until the classes began. I don't remember what we talked about, but it felt like we connected on a deep soul level. When I looked into his clear blue eyes, it felt like time stopped. As we shook hands to say "goodbye," he asked, "How can I get in touch with you?" I jotted my email and telephone number on a piece of paper and handed it to him.

"I look forward to hearing from you," I said.

"Oh, you'll be hearing from me."

I saw my friend Susan before I left and told her what happened. I drove home from the conference on cloud nine. *This has to be God,* I thought.

My friend Susan called the next day and asked, "Are you sitting down?"

"Why, what's the matter?"

"I have some bad news. Mark told me when the conference was over that he's been diagnosed with cancer and has a 50-50 chance of living. He's being operated on next week."

"You have to be kidding. When did he find out?" I asked.

"He found out a couple of weeks ago. He decided to come to the conference because he didn't want to be alone. I'm sorry Pat."

I felt disappointed, sad and angry.

God, why did he ask me for my number if he didn't have any intention of calling me? I don't understand. I really thought you were opening a door.

The anger passed quickly, replaced by compassion and love. God placed him on my heart and I prayed for him daily. I didn't know him and yet felt pain when I thought about him. Was this a GODincidence and only meant for me to pray and intercede for him? I trusted that if I was supposed to meet him again, he would call and it would be clear that God opened the door. I bought a get well card to send him, but didn't have his address. And neither did my friend Susan. I called the state college he worked at, but they wouldn't give me his address. God closed the door and had other plans for me and him.

Today, I'm at peace and grateful for being single and all the healing that's taken place within my heart. I appreciate and cherish my life, the quiet time and the freedom to do whatever I want with whom I want. Being single has forced me (sometimes kicking and screaming) to take responsibility for myself, to get to know myself and look within for my answers, as well as ask questions when I don't know something (and that's okay to not know everything.) I no longer put my head in the sand and say I can't do something, when in reality I can when I try. My father's favorite saying was: FIND YOURSELF. I know today it's more than that. It's also KNOW YOURSELF AND BE YOURSELF.

God has given me the desire of my heart to meet my soul mate. He will fulfill it in His time and in His way. God wanted me to stop trying so hard and allow Him to bring my soul mate to me. Daily I pray the affirmation,

My soul mate is lovingly and effortlessly coming into my life

I received an email from my cousin one day. God has a sense of humor and loves to make me laugh. This is a woman's story of how she met her soul mate:

"Wrong Funeral" and God is not sleeping!

"Consumed by my loss, I didn't notice the hardness of the pew where I sat. I was at the funeral of my dearest friend - my mother. She finally had her long battle with cancer over. The hurt was so intense, I found it hard to breathe at times. Always supportive, mother clapped loudest at my school plays, held a box of tissues while listening to my first heartbreak, comforted me at my father's death and encouraged me my entire life.

"When mother's illness was diagnosed, my sister had a new baby and my brother recently married, so it fell on me, the twenty seven year old middle child without entanglements to take care of her. I felt it an honor. "What now, Lord?" I asked sitting in church, my life stretched out before me as an empty abyss.

"My brother sat stoically with his face toward the cross while clutching his wife's hand. My sister sat slumped against her husband's shoulder, his arms around her as she cradled their child. All so deeply grieving, no one noticed I sat alone. My place had been with my mother, preparing meals, helping her walk, taking her to the doctor, reading the bible together. Now she was with the Lord. My work was finished and I was alone.

"I heard a door open and slam shut at the back of the church. Quick footsteps hurried along the carpeted floor. An exasperated young man looked around briefly and then sat next to me. He folded his hands and placed them on his lap. His eyes were brimming with tears. He began to sniffle. "I'm late," he explained, though no explanation was necessary. After several eulogies, he leaned over and commented. "Why do they keep calling Mary by the name of Margaret?"

"Because that was her name, Margaret, never Mary, no one called her Mary," I whispered. I wondered why this person couldn't have sat on the other side of the church. He interrupted my grieving with his tears and fidgeting. Who was this stranger anyway?

"No, that isn't correct," he insisted, as several people looked at us whispering. "Her name is Mary, Mary Peters."

"That isn't who this is."

"Isn't this the Lutheran church?"

"No, the Lutheran church is across the street. I believe you're at the wrong funeral, sir."

"The solemnity of the occasion mixed with the realization of the man's mistake bubbled up inside me and came out as laughter. I cupped my hands over my face, hoping it would be interpreted as sobs. The creaking pew gave me away. Sharp looks from other mourners only made the situation seem more hilarious. I peeked at the bewildered misguided man seated next to me. He was laughing, too, as he glanced around, deciding it was too late for an uneventful exit.

"I imagined mother laughing. At the final "Amen" we darted out a door and into the parking lot. "I do believe we will be the talk of the town" he smiled. He said his name was Rick and since he had missed his aunt's funeral, he asked me out for a cup of coffee. That afternoon began a lifelong journey for me with this man who attended the wrong funeral, but was in the right place.

A year later we were married and have been married for twenty five years.

(This text was emailed to me and I have been unable to locate its source or determine any copywrite for the material. Any copywrite brought to the author's attention and proven, will be corrected in the next printing of the book and given correct attribution. Please forgive any error of omission.)

After reading that beautiful story, it confirmed what God was saying to me through my prayer and dreams. God wants me to live my life to the fullest, trusting His timing and wisdom. God wants me to be happy and content right where I'm at. He wants me to appreciate what I have now with expectant faith and anticipation of what is to come. I'm trusting God to do something as magnificent as the funeral story because he knows how much I love surprises and WOWS.

His plan is perfect. I continue to pray and visualize my soul mate coming into my life. What I think about and thank about, I bring about. When I visualize, I materialize. I see in my mind's eye the end results and "feel" like it's already happened. I see my soul mate and I walking on the beach, having fun, praying together. If God allows me to see it, I can trust He will bring it about.

I'll have to write another book to share how God brings my soul mate into my life, unless He has other plans and brings my soul mate to me before I finish the book. I know it will be a wonderful story, no matter what, and it will be worth the wait.

✤ My life is unfolding according to a Divine plan

✤ I radiate my heart's desire and attract my soul mate into my life

✤ I open my heart and soul to receive my soul mate

✤ I deliberately and boldly attract my soul mate into my life

I Am a Woman Giving Birth to Myself

JOURNAL PAGE

How do I surrender to the God within and
become spiritually fulfilled?

_____

_____

_____

_____

_____

_____

_____

_____

_____

_____

_____

_____

_____

_____

_____

_____

_____

_____

~ *Epilogue* ~

My manuscript was complete and ready to be sent to the publisher. While in prayer on Mother's Day, I asked God to speak to me through the angels about my future for my book. I randomly chose an angel card from the Angelic Messenger cards. (Young- Sowers 1993)

ABUNDANCE.

"You have a vision for your life that has grown from your heart and spirit, a vision that tells you that you are a child of the universe and are meant to grow in love, wisdom and a cooperative spirit. You are meant to use your creativity, imagination, and abilities to the fullest extent in order to create a magnificent Earth home for you, those you love, and all the human beings and creatures in your planetary family. Perhaps you'll find that abundance flows most directly from an attitude appreciating what you already have." (Young-Sowers 1993)

I wrote in my journal that day, "My heart overflows with joy and gratefulness for the divine energy I feel flowing through me." I felt alive and excited about the next step with my book. After seven years of writing, it was finally going to be born. Being Mother's Day, I prayed to feel my mother's presence and maybe even hear the song, *Honey.*

That afternoon, I shopped for Mother's Day plants at Seven Arrows Herb Farm where my daughter Mary works. The owner of the shop, Judy said to a customer, "Gary, do you know Pat? She's Mary's mother and she just wrote a book."

"No, I don't think I do."

I reached out my hand and introduced myself.

"Hi, I'm Pat Hastings, nice to meet you Gary."

"What's the name of your book?" he asked.

"Simply a Woman of Faith."

"I like the title." After telling him a little bit about myself and the journey writing my book, he reached into his pocket and handed me his business card.

"Send me your book. I'd like to read it and give you feedback. My wife will read it too."

"Thank you."

Gary appeared eager and sincere to help. I sensed he was a spiritual man by the twinkle in his eyes and big smile when he shook my hand. As an active member of the community, Gary wore many hats. In short, he knew many people.

"What do you know about marketing?" I asked.

He smiled and said, "I'm definitely a networker."

I sensed in my spirit this was another GODincidence and that Gary was going to help me with the next step for my book – marketing and getting it out there. Although I didn't hear the song *Honey* on the radio, I have a feeling my mom had something to do with this chance meeting.

As I reflected on my day that evening, I heard the small still voice of God say:

THIS IS THE BEGINNING. REJOICE, PAT. YOU HAVE SAID YES AND TAKEN A RISK NOT ONLY WITH YOUR TIME AND ENERGY, BUT WITH YOUR MONEY. I AM BLESSING YOU AND GOING BEFORE YOU TO OPEN DOORS. I WILL BRING PEOPLE TO HELP YOU WITH THE NEXT STEP OF PUBLISHING AND PROMOTING YOUR BOOK. TRUST ME. ALL YOU HAVE TO DO IS KEEP WALKING IN FAITH, SAYING YES TO YOUR SOUL AND INTUITION.

Quick Order Form

SATISFACTION GUARANTEED

Web orders: www.simplyawomanoffaith.com

Amazon.com
BarnesandNoble.com

Books can be purchased or ordered at:

Positive New Beginnings
401- 432-7195
Email address
womanoffaith@bluebottle.com

See our web site www.simplyawomanoffaith.com for FREE newsletter, articles, retreats, workshops.